NAUTICAL
KNITS
for
KIDS

Debbie Bliss

NAUTICAL KNITS *for* KIDS

Trafalgar Square Publishing

*This book is dedicated to the
life of Thomas Oku-Watton.
A child of light.*

First published in the United States of America in 1998 by
Trafalgar Square Publishing, North Pomfret, Vermont 05053

First published in Great Britain in 1998
by Collins & Brown Limited

Printed and bound in Spain by Graficromo

1 3 5 7 9 8 6 4 2

ISBN 1-57076-107-8

Library of Congress Catalog Card Number: 97-61779

Editor: Margot Richardson
Designer: Carole Perks
Photography: Sandra Lousada

Reproduction by Grafiscan

Contents

Introduction

Nautical Knits for Kids is my latest collection of handknits for children with 25 designs all inspired by the sights and sounds of the sea. Most of us have wonderful memories of childhood holidays at the coast: golden days of buckets and spades, trips around the bay and picnics on the beach. I wanted to capture the spirit of escape and holiday in *Nautical Knits* and to pay homage to the classic perfection of traditional Arans and fisher knits by using their cabling, guernsey stitch patterns and lace panelling – and giving them a contemporary twist.

I have combined Aran stitches with nautical motifs, worked guernseys in gradually fading denim yarns and used delicate lace patterns that echo the beautiful fisher jerseys from the island of Eriskay in the Hebrides. I have ensured that the designs cover all knitting abilities, and there are basic one-colour tops and simple stripes for the beginner.

Depending on the style, I have given the knits generous size allowances, as I feel not only should children feel comfortable and unrestricted in knits, but now that knitting is a labour of lover rather than economy, there should be room for growth. However, if you prefer a less generous look, check the actual measurements of the pattern you want to knit: you can always knit the size below.

Working with my favourite photographer, Sandra Lousada, who captured the spirit and essence of the children so beautifully on sun-filled beaches, *Nautical Knits for Kids* has been a great adventure. I hope you will experience the same pleasure in knitting up the designs.

Debbie Bliss

Simple Tunic with Hood
page 41

Red and Cream Striped Top
page 42

Simple Sweater with Cable Detail page 43

Denim Sweater with Hearts page 44

Sailor-collared Jacket

page 45

Eyelet Lace Cardigan

page 47

Star Sweater page 49

Union Jack Sweater page 50

Cream Fisherman Shirt

page 52

Aran Cardigan with
Saddle Shoulders

page 54

**Multicoloured
Sweater**
page 56

Tartan and Boats Cardigan
page 57

Lace Fisher Jersey
page 58

Black and White Cable Sweater

page 63

Entrelac Sweater

page 64

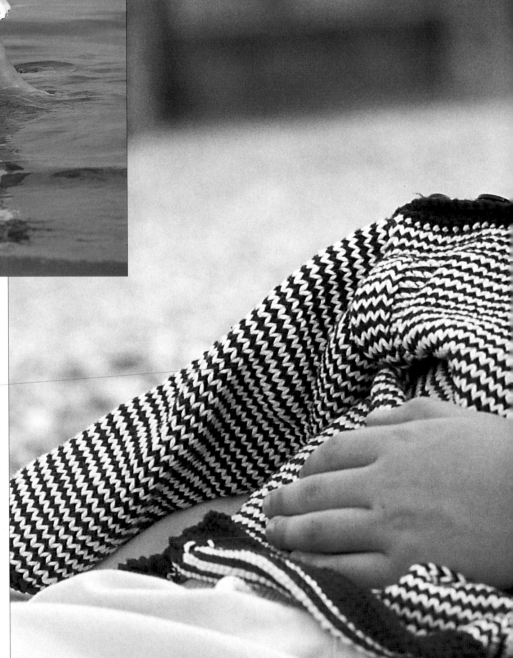

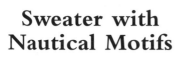

**Sweater with
Nautical Motifs**
page 71

**Guernsey
Tunic Dress**

page 74

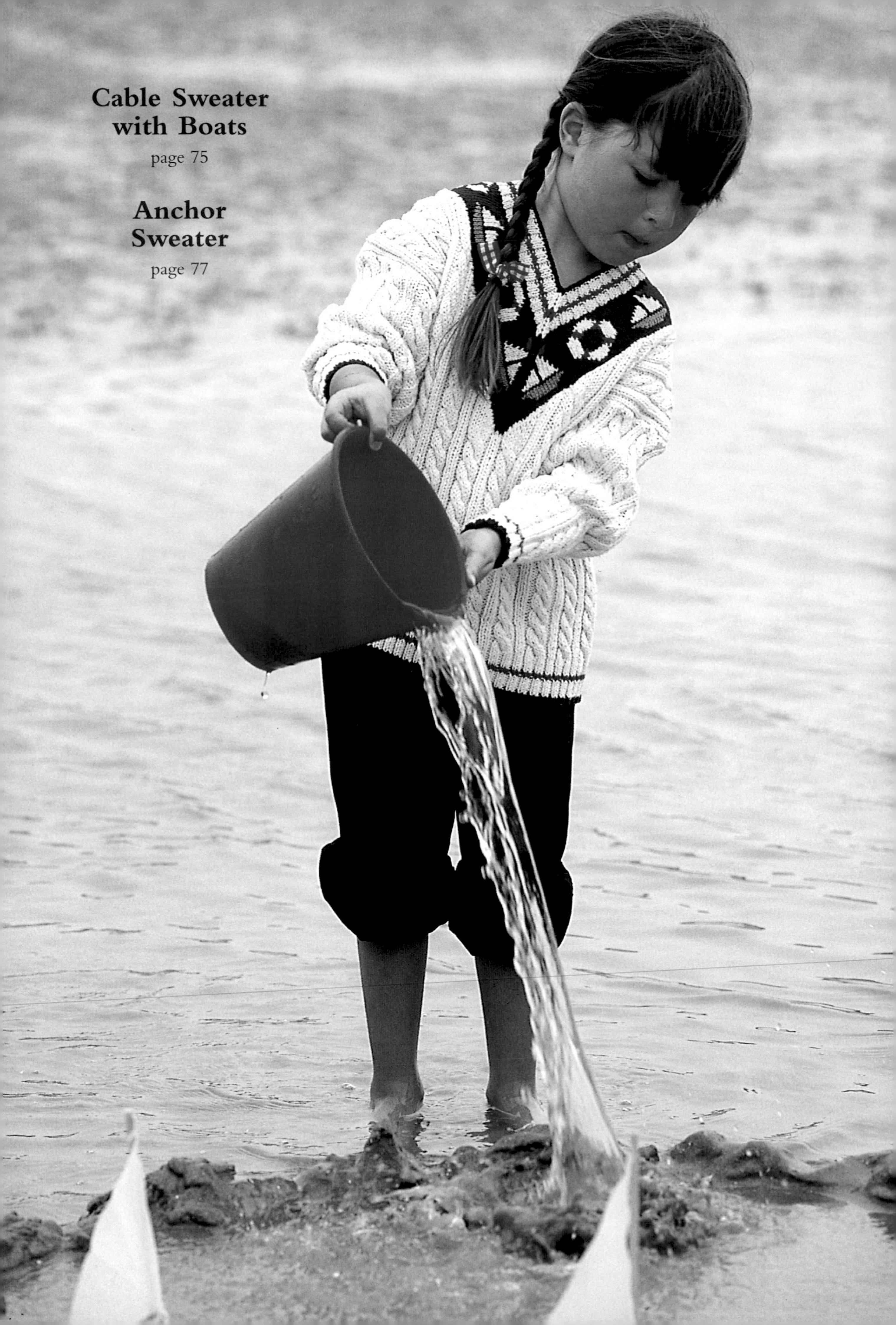

Cable Sweater with Boats

page 75

Anchor Sweater

page 77

Basic Information

NOTES

Figures for larger sizes are given in ( ) brackets. Where only one figure appears, this applies to all sizes.

Work figures given in [ ] brackets the number of times stated afterwards. Alternatively, they give the resultant number of stitches.

Where 0 appears, no stitches or rows are worked for this size.

The yarn amounts given in the instructions are based on average requirements and should therefore be considered approximate. If you want to use a substitute yarn, choose a yarn of the same type and weight as the one recommended. The following descriptions of the various Rowan yarns are meant as a guide to the yarn weight and type (i.e. cotton, wool, etc.). Remember that the description of the yarn weight is only a rough guide and you should always test a yarn first to see if it will achieve the correct tension (gauge).

Cotton Glace: a lightweight cotton yarn (100% cotton) approx. 112m/123yd per 50g/1¼oz ball.

Handknit DK Cotton: a medium-weight cotton yarn (100% cotton) approx. 85m/90yd per 50g/1¼oz ball.

The amount of a substitute yarn needed is determined by the number of metres/yards needed rather than by the number of grams/ounces. If you are unsure when choosing a suitable substitute, ask your yarn shop to advise you.

Rowan Denim: (100% cotton) approx. 93m/102yd per 50g/1¼oz ball.
Unlike any other yarn, Rowan Denim will shrink and fade when it is washed, just like a pair of jeans. Unlike many 'denim look' yarns this uses real indigo dye which only coats the surface of the yarn, leaving a white core that is gradually exposed through washing and wearing. When washed for the first time the yarn will shrink by up to one-fifth on length; but the width will remain the same.

All the necessary adjustments have been made in the instructions for the patterns specially designed for Denim so these patterns should not be knitted in any other yarn.
The knitted pieces should be washed separately at a temperature of 60-70°C (140-158°F) before sewing the garment together. The pieces can then be tumble-dried. Dye loss will be greatest during the initial wash; the appearance of the garment will, however, be greatly enhanced with additional washing and wearing. The cream denim yarn will shrink in the same way but will not fade.

TENSION

Each pattern in this book specifies a tension - the number of stitches and rows per centimetre/inch that should be obtained with the given needles, yarn and stitch pattern. Check your tension carefully before commencing work.

Use the same yarn, needles and stitch pattern as those to be used for the main work and knit a sample at least 12.5cm/5in square. Smooth out the finished sample on a flat surface but do not stretch it. To check the tension, place a ruler horizontally on the sample and mark 10cm/4in across with pins. Count the number of stitches between the pins. To check the row tension, place a ruler vertically on the sample and mark 10cm/4in with pins. Count the number of rows between the pins. If the number of stitches and rows is greater than specified, try again using larger needles; if less, use smaller needles.

The stitch tension is the most important element to get right.

The following terms may be unfamiliar to US readers.

UK terms	US terms
ball band	*yarn wrapper*
cast off	*bind off*
DK wool	*knitting worsted yarn*
Make up (garment)	*finish (garment)*
rib	*ribbing*
stocking stitch	*stockinette stitch*
tension	*gauge*
slipover	*vest*

In the US balls or hanks of yarn are sold in ounces, not in grams; the weights of the relevant Rowan yarns are given on this page.

In addition, a few specific knitting terms may be unfamiliar to some readers. The list below explains the abbreviations used in this book to help the reader understand how to follow the various stitches and stages.

STANDARD ABBREVIATIONS

alt = alternate; **beg** = begin(ning); **cont** = continue; **dec** = decreas(e)ing; **foll** = following; **inc** = increas(e)ing; **k** = knit; **m1** = make one by picking up loop lying between st just worked and next st and work into the back of it; **patt** = pattern; **p** = purl; **psso** = pass slipped st over; **rem** = remain(ing); **rep** = repeat; **skpo** = sl one, k1, pass slipped st over; **sl** = slip; **st(s)** = stitch(es); **st st** = stocking stitch; **tbl** = through back of loop(s); **tog** = together; **yb** = yarn back, **yf** = yarn forward; **yon** = yarn over needle; **yrn** = yarn round needle.

IMPORTANT

Check on ball band for washing instructions. After washing, pat garments into shape and dry flat away from direct heat.

Simple Tunic with Hood page 10

MATERIALS

8(9:10) 50g balls of Rowan Cotton Glace.
Pair each of 2¾mm (No 12/US 2) and 3¼mm (No 10/US 3) knitting needles.

MEASUREMENTS

To fit age	2	3	4	years
Actual chest	73	78	83	cm
measurement	29	31	32½	in
Length	40	43	46	cm
	15¾	17	18	in
Sleeve seam	24	28	31	cm
	9½	11	12	in

TENSION

25 sts and 34 rows to 10cm/4in square over st st on 3¼mm (No 10/US 3) needles.

ABBREVIATIONS

See page 40.

BACK

With 2¾mm (No 12/US 2) needles cast on 92(98:104) sts.
K 7 rows.
Change to 3¼mm (No 10/US 3) needles.
1st row (right side) K.
2nd row K5, p to last 5 sts, k5.
Rep last 2 rows 3 times more.
Beg with a k row, work in st st until Back measures 24(25:26)cm/9½(10: 10¼)in from beg, ending with a p row.
Next row K5, p6, k to last 11 sts, p6, k5.
Next row P. ★★
Rep last 2 rows until Back measures 40(43:46)cm/15¾(17:18)in from beg, ending with a wrong side row.
Shape Shoulders
Cast off 24(26:28) sts at beg of next 2 rows. Cast off rem 44(46:48) sts.

FRONT

Work as given for Back to ★★. Rep last 2 rows until Front measures 34(37:39)cm/13½(14¾:15¼)in from beg, ending with a wrong side row.
Shape Neck
Next row Patt 37(39:41), cast off next 18(20:22) sts, patt to end.
Work on last set of sts only. Dec one st at neck edge on next 10 rows, then on 3 foll alt rows. 24(26:28) sts. Cont straight for a few rows until Front matches Back to shoulder shaping, ending at side edge. Cast off.
With wrong side facing, rejoin yarn to rem sts and patt to end. Complete as first side.

SLEEVES

With 2¾mm (No 12/US 2) needles cast on 38(42:42) sts.
1st rib row (right side) K2, [p2, k2] to end.
2nd rib row P2, [k2, p2] to end.
Rib 14 rows more, inc 6(4:6) sts evenly across last row. 44(46:48) sts.
Change to 3¼mm (No 10/US 3) needles.
Beg with a k row, work in st st, inc one st at each end of 1st row and every foll

2nd(2nd:3rd) row until there are 70(64:68) sts, then on every foll 3rd row until there are 90(94:98) sts. Cont straight until Sleeve measures 24(28:31)cm/9½(11:12)in from beg. Cast off.

HOOD

With 3¼mm (No 10/US 3) needles cast on 47(51:55) sts.
Next row (right side) K.
Next row K5, p to end.
Rep last 2 rows until Hood measures approximately 46(51:55)cm/18(20:21½)in from beg, ending with a wrong side row. Cast off.

TO MAKE UP

Join shoulder seams. Sew on sleeves, placing centre of sleeves to shoulder seams. Join sleeve seams and side seams to top of garter st borders. Fold hood in half lengthwise and join back seam. Sew hood in place.

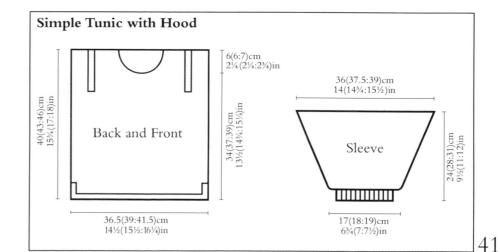

Simple Tunic with Hood

Back and Front
40(43:46)cm 15¾(17:18)in
34(37:39)cm 13½(14¾:15¼)in
6(6:7)cm 2¼(2¼:2¾)in
36.5(39:41.5)cm 14½(15½:16¼)in

Sleeve
36(37.5:39)cm 14(14¾:15½)in
24(28:31)cm 9½(11:12)in
17(18:19)cm 6¾(7:7½)in

Red and Cream Striped Top   page 11

MATERIALS

5(6:6) 50g balls of Rowan Cotton
Glace in Red (A).
4(5:5) balls in Cream (B).
Pair each of 2¾mm (No 12/US 2)
and 3¼mm (No 10/US 3) knitting
needles.

MEASUREMENTS

To fit age	2	3	4	years
Actual chest	73	78	83	cm
measurement	28½	30½	32½	in
Length	38	42	46	cm
	15	16½	18	in
Sleeve seam	24	28	31	cm
	9½	11	12¼	in

TENSION

25 sts and 34 rows to 10cm/4in square
over st st on 3¼mm (No 10/US 3)
needles.

ABBREVIATIONS

See page 40.

BACK

With 2¾mm (No 12/US 2) needles and
A, cast on 92(98:104) sts.
K 7 rows.
Change to 3¼mm (No 10/US 3) needles.
Change to B.
1st row (right side) K.
2nd row K5, p to last 5 sts, k5.
Change to A and rep last 2 rows once.
Change to B and rep 1st and 2nd rows once.

Beg with a k row, work in st st and stripe
patt of 4 rows A, 2 rows B, 2 rows A and 2
rows B throughout until Back measures
38(42:46)cm/15(16½:18)in from beg,
ending with a wrong side row.
Shape Shoulders
Cast off 26(28:30) sts at beg of next
2 rows. Leave rem 40(42:44) sts on
a holder.

FRONT

Work as given for Back until Front
measures 28(31:34)cm/11(12¼:13¼)in
from beg, ending with a wrong side row.
Shape Neck
Next row Patt 46(49:52), turn.
Work on this set of sts only. Dec one st at
neck edge on every row until 34(39:42) sts
rem, then on every alt row until 26(28:30)
sts rem. Cont straight until Front matches
Back to shoulder shaping, ending at side
edge. Cast off.
With right side facing, rejoin yarn to rem
sts and patt to end. Complete as first side.

SLEEVES

With 2¾mm (No 12/US 2) needles and
A, cast on 38(42:42) sts.
1st rib row (right side) K2, [p2, k2]
to end.
2nd rib row P2, [k2, p2] to end.
Cont in rib, work in stripe patt of 2 rows
A, 4 rows B, 4 rows A and 4 rows B, inc
6(4:6) sts evenly across last row.
44(46:48) sts.
Change to 3¼mm (No 10/US 3) needles.
Beg with a k row, work in st st and stripe
patt of 4 rows A, 2 rows B, 2 rows A, 2
rows B, **at the same time**, inc one st at
each end of 1st row and every foll 2nd
row until there are 74(68:68) sts, then on
every foll 3rd row until there are
92(98:104) sts. Cont straight until Sleeve
measures 24(28:31)cm/9½(11:12¼)in from
beg. Cast off.

COLLAR

Join shoulder seams.
Right side With 3¼mm (No 10/
US 3) needles and B, cast on 30(32:34) sts.
Beg with a k row, work in st st and stripe
patt of 2 rows B, 2 rows A, 2 rows B, 4
rows A throughout, **at the same time**,
cast off 2 sts at beg of next row and every
foll alt row until 6 sts rem. Work 1 row.
Cast off. Sew shaped edge of right side of
collar to right front neck.
Left side Cast on and work in st st and
stripe patt as given for right side, **at the
same time,** cast off 2 sts at beg of 2nd
row and every foll alt row until 6 sts rem.
Cast off. Sew shaped edge of left side of
collar to left front neck.
Back collar With 3¼mm (No 10/
US 3) needles, A and beg at outside edge
of left side of collar, k up 20(22:24) sts
along top edge of collar, k back neck sts, k
up 20(22:24) sts across top edge of right
side of collar, ending at outside edge.
80(86:92) sts.
P 1 row.
Beg with a k row, work in st st and stripe
patt of 2 rows B, 2 rows A, 2 rows B and 4
rows A for 36(46:56) rows.
Change to 2¾mm (No 12/US 2) needles.
With A, k 6 rows, inc one st at each end of
every wrong side row. Cast off.
Side edgings With 2¾mm (No 12/ US
2) needles and A, k up 56(64:72) sts along
one outside edge of collar. K 5 rows, inc
one st at each end of every wrong side
row. Cast off.
Work other side in same way.

TO MAKE UP

Sew on sleeves, placing centre of sleeves
to shoulder seams. Join sleeve seams and
side seams to top of garter st borders.
Mitre back corners of collar edgings.
Fold over front ends of edging and secure
in position.

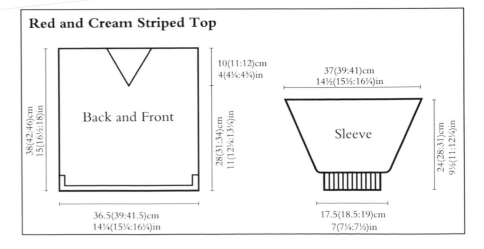

Red and Cream Striped Top

Back and Front
38(42:46)cm / 15(16½:18)in
28(31:34)cm / 11(12¼:13¼)in
10(11:12)cm / 4(4¼:4¾)in
36.5(39:41.5)cm / 14¼(15¼:16¼)in

Sleeve
37(39:41)cm / 14½(15½:16¼)in
24(28:31)cm / 9½(11:12¼)in
17.5(18.5:19)cm / 7(7¼:7½)in

Simple Sweater with Cable Detail page 12

MATERIALS

7(8:10) 50g balls of Rowan DK
Handknit Cotton.
Pair each of 3¼mm (No 10/US 3)
and 4mm (No 8/US 6) knitting
needles.
Cable needle.

MEASUREMENTS

To fit age	1-2	2-3	4-5	years
Actual chest	71	80	91	cm
measurement	28	31½	36	in
Length	36	42	48	cm
	14¼	16½	19	in
Sleeve seam	20	24	28	cm
	8	9½	11	in

TENSION

20 sts and 28 rows to 10cm/4in square
over st st on 4mm (No 8/US 6)
needles.

ABBREVIATIONS

C4F = sl next 2 sts onto cable needle
and leave at front of work, k2, then k2
from cable needle.
Also see page 40.

BACK

With 3¼mm (No 10/US 3) needles cast
on 82(90:98) sts.
1st rib row (right side) K2, [p1, k4, p1,
k2] to end.
2nd rib row P2, [k1, p4, k1, p2] to end.
3rd rib row K2, [p1, C4F, p1, k2] to end.
4th row As 2nd row.
Rep last 4 rows 2(3:3) times more.
Change to 4mm (No 8/US 6) needles.
Next row K0(8:0), k2 tog, [k6(6:14), k2
tog] to last 0(8:0) sts, k0(8:0). 71(80:91) sts.
Beg with a p row, work in st st until Back
measures 25(30:36)cm/10(11¾:14¼)in
from beg, ending with a p row.
Next row K6, p2, k4, p2, k to last 14 sts,
p2, k4, p2, k6.
Next row P6, k2, p4, k2, p to last 14 sts,
k2, p4, k2, p6.
Next row K6, p2, C4F, p2, k to last 14 sts,
p2, C4F, p2, k6.
Next row P6, k2, p4, k2, p to last 14 sts,
k2, p4, k2, p6.
Rep last 4 rows 3 times more. ★★
Beg with a k row, work in st st across all
sts until Back measures 36(42: 48)cm/14¼
(16½:19)in from beg, ending with a p row.
Shape Shoulders
Cast off 8(10:12) sts at beg of next 2 rows
and 9(10:12) sts at beg of next 2 rows.
Leave rem 37(40:43) sts on a holder.

FRONT

Work as given for Back to ★★. Beg with a
k row, work 4 rows in st st.
Shape Neck
Next row K27(30:34), turn.
Work on this set of sts only. Dec one st at
neck edge on every row until 17(20:24) sts
rem. Cont straight for a few rows until
Front matches Back to shoulder shaping,
ending at side edge.
Shape Shoulder
Cast off 8(10:12) sts at beg of next row.
Work 1 row. Cast off rem 9(10:12) sts.
With right side facing, slip centre
17(20:23) sts onto a holder, rejoin yarn to
rem sts, k to end.
Complete to match first side.

SLEEVES

With 3¼mm (No 10/US 3) needles cast
on 34(34:42) sts.
Work 12(16:16) rows in rib as given for
Back welt, inc 8(12:6) sts evenly across last
row. 42(46:48) sts.
Change to 4mm (No 8/US 6) needles.
Beg with a k row, work in st st, inc one st
at each end of 3rd row and every foll 4th
row until there are 60(70:74) sts. Cont
straight until Sleeve measures
20(24:28)cm/8(9½:11)in from beg.
Cast off.

NECKBAND

Join right shoulder seam.
With 3¼mm (No 10/US 3) needles and
right side facing, k up 11(15:16) sts down
left front neck, k centre front neck sts inc
3(4:3) sts, k up 11(15:16) sts up right front
neck, k back neck sts inc 3(3:5) sts.
82(97:106) sts.
Next row K0(1:0), [p2, k1, p4, k1] to last
2(0:2) sts, p2(0:2).
Next row K2(0:2), [p1, C4F, p1, k2] to
last 0(1:0) st, p0(1:0).
Next row K0(1:0), [p2, k1, p4, k1] to last
2(0:2) sts, p2(0:2).
Next row K2(0:2), [p1, k4, p1, k2] to last
0(1:0) st, p0(1:0).
Rep last 4 rows 1(2:2) times more, then
work first 3 rows again. Cast off in patt.

TO MAKE UP

Join left shoulder and neckband seam. Sew
on sleeves, placing centre of sleeves to
shoulder seams. Join side and sleeve seams.

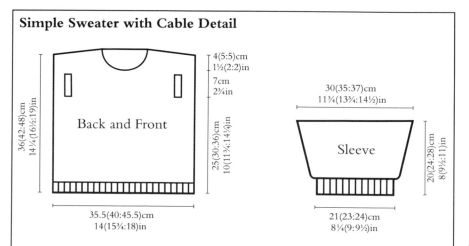

Simple Sweater with Cable Detail

Back and Front

Sleeve

36(42:48)cm
14¼(16½:19)in

25(30:36)cm
10(11¾:14¼)in

4(5:5)cm
1½(2:2)in

7cm
2¾in

35.5(40:45.5)cm
14(15¾:18)in

30(35:37)cm
11¾(13¾:14½)in

21(23:24)cm
8¼(9:9½)in

20(24:28)cm
8(9½:11)in

Denim Sweater with Hearts   page 13

MATERIALS

8(9:10) 50g balls of Rowan Denim (see page 40).
Pair each of 3¾mm (No 9/US 4) and 4mm (No 8/US 6) knitting needles.
Cable needle.

MEASUREMENTS

To fit age	1	2	3	years

The following measurements are after the garment has been washed according to the instructions given on ball band.

Actual chest	69	77	85	cm
measurement	27	30½	33½	in
Length	36	40	44	cm
	14¼	15¾	17¼	in
Sleeve seam	21	23	25	cm
	8¼	9	10	in

TENSION

20 sts and 28 rows to 10cm/4in square over st st on 4mm (No 8/US 6) needles before washing.

ABBREVIATIONS

C3B = sl next st onto cable needle and leave at back of work, k2, then k1 from cable needle;
C3F = sl next 2 sts onto cable needle and leave at front of work, k1, then k2 from cable needle;
Cr3L = sl next 2 sts onto cable needle and leave at front of work, p1, then k2 from cable needle;
Cr3R = sl next st onto cable needle and leave at back of work, k2, then p1 from cable needle;
Cr4L = sl next 2 sts onto cable needle and leave at front of work, p2, then k2 from cable needle;
Cr4R = sl next 2 sts onto cable needle and leave at back of work, k2, then p2 from cable needle;
mb = [k1, p1] twice in next st, turn, p4, turn, sl 2, k2 tog, pass 2 slipped sts over;
Tw3 = sl next st onto cable needle and leave at front of work, k2, then k1 from cable needle.
Also see page 40.

PANEL A

Worked over 8 sts.
1st row (right side) P2, mb, p1, Cr3R, p1.
2nd row K2, p2, k4.
3rd row P3, Cr3R, p2.
4th row K3, p2, k3.
5th row P2, Cr3R, p3.
6th row K4, p2, k2,
7th row P1, Cr3R, p4.
8th row K5, p2, k1.
9th row P1, Cr3L, p1, mb, p2.
10th row As 6th row.
11th row P2, Cr3L, p3.
12th row As 4th row.
13th row P3, Cr3L, p2.
14th row As 2nd row.
15th row P4, Cr3L, p1.
16th row K1, p2, k5.
These 16 rows form patt.

PANEL B

Worked over 37 sts.
1st row (right side) K6, p1, k1, p7, Cr3R, k1, Cr3L, p7, k1, p1, k6.
2nd row P5, k1, p2, k7, p3, k1, p3, k7, p2, k1, p5.
3rd row K4, [p1, k1] twice, p6, C3B, p1, k1, p1, C3F, p6, [k1, p1] twice, k4.
4th row P3, k1, p1, k1, p2, k6, p2, k1, [p1, k1] twice, p2, k6, p2, k1, p1, k1, p3.
5th row K2, [p1, k1] 3 times, p5, Cr3R, k1, [p1, k1] twice, Cr3L, p5, [k1, p1] 3 times, k2.
6th row [P1, k1] 3 times, p2, k5, p3, k1, [p1, k1] twice, p3, k5, p2, [k1, p1] 3 times.
7th row K2, [p1, k1] 3 times, p4, C3B, p1, [k1, p1] 3 times, C3F, p4, [k1, p1] 3 times, k2.
8th row P3, k1, p1, k1, p2, k4, p2, k1, [p1, k1] 4 times, p2, k4, p2, k1, p1, k1, p3.
9th row K4, [p1, k1] twice, p3, Cr3R, k1, [p1, k1] 4 times, Cr3L, p3, [k1, p1] twice, k4.
10th row P5, k1, p2, k3, p3, k1, [p1, k1] 4 times, p3, k3, p2, k1, p5.
11th row K6, p1, k1, p2, C3B, p1, [k1, p1] 5 times, C3F, p2, k1, p1, k6.
12th row P5, k1, p2, k2, p2, k1, [p1, k1] 6 times, p2, k2, p2, k1, p5.
13th row K4, [p1, k1] twice, p1, Cr3R, k1, [p1, k1] 6 times, Cr3L, p1, [k1, p1] twice, k4.
14th row P3, k1, p1, k1, p2, k1, p3, k1, [p1, k1] 6 times, p3, k1, p2, k1, p1, k1, p3.
15th row K2, [p1, k1] 3 times, p1, k2, p1, [k1, p1] 7 times, k2, p1, [k1, p1] 3 times, k2.
16th row [P1, k1] 3 times, p2, k1, p3, k1, [p1, k1] 6 times, p3, k1, p2, [k1, p1] 3 times.
17th row K2, [p1, k1] 3 times, p1, Cr4L, p1, [k1, p1] 5 times, Cr4R, p1, [k1, p1] 3 times, k2.
18th row P3, k1, p1, k1, p2, k3, p3, k1, [p1, k1] 4 times, p3, k3, p2, k1, p1, k1, p3.

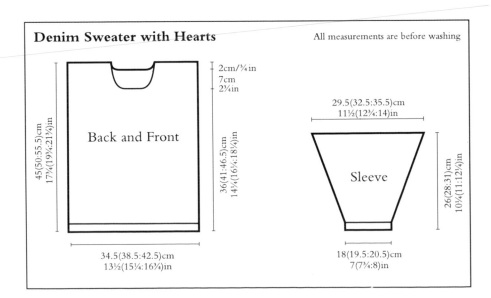

Denim Sweater with Hearts   All measurements are before washing

Back and Front

45(50:55.5)cm
17¾(19¾:21¾)in

2cm/¾in
7cm
2¾in

36(41:46.5)cm
14¼(16¼:18¼)in

34.5(38.5:42.5)cm
13½(15¼:16¾)in

29.5(32.5:35.5)cm
11½(12¾:14)in

Sleeve

26(28:31)cm
10¼(11:12¼)in

18(19.5:20.5)cm
7(7¾:8)in

19th row K4, [p1, k1] twice, p3, Cr4L, p1, k1, p1, mb, p1, k1, p1, Cr4R, p3, [k1, p1] twice, k4.
20th row P5, k1, p2, k8, p2, k1, p2, k8, p2, k1, p5.
These 20 rows form patt.

BACK
With 3¾mm (No 9/US 4) needles cast on 75(83:91) sts.
1st row P1, [k1, p1] to end.
This row forms moss st. Moss st 8 rows more.
Next row Moss st 17(21:25), m1, moss st 18, m1, moss st 5, m1, moss st 18, m1, moss st to end. 79(87:95) sts.
Change to 4mm (No 8/US 6) needles.
1st row (right side) *Moss st 5(7:9), sl 1 purlwise, k2, moss st 5(7:9)*; work 1st row of panel A and panel B, then 9th row of panel A, rep from * to *.
2nd row *Moss st 5(7:9), sl 1 purlwise, p2, moss st 5(7:9)*; work 10th row of panel A, then 2nd row of panel B and panel A, rep from * to *.
3rd row Moss st 5(7:9), Tw3, moss st 5(7:9), work 3rd row of panel A and panel B, then 11th row of panel A, moss st 5(7:9), sl next 2 sts onto cable needle and leave at back of work, k1, then k2 from cable needle, moss st 5(7:9).
4th row *Moss st 5(7:9), p3, moss st 5(7:9)*; work 12th row of panel A, then 4th row of panel B and panel A, rep from * to *.
These 4 rows set position of panels and form cable patt at side edges.** Patt a further 116(130:146) rows.
Shape Neck
Next row Patt 27(30:33), turn.
Work on this set of sts only. Keeping patt correct, cast off 2 sts at beg of next row and 2 foll alt rows. Cast off rem 21(24:27) sts.
With right side facing, slip centre 25(27:29) sts onto a holder, rejoin yarn to rem sts, patt to end. Patt 1 row. Complete as first side.

FRONT
Work as given for Back to **. Patt a further 96(110:126) rows.
Shape Neck
Next row Patt 32(35:38), turn.
Work on this set of sts only. Dec one st at neck edge on next 11 rows. 21(24:27) sts.
Patt 14 rows straight. Cast off.
With right side facing, slip centre 15(17:19) sts onto a holder, rejoin yarn to rem sts, patt to end. Complete as first side.

SLEEVES
With 3¾mm (No 9/US 4) needles cast on 41(43: 45) sts. Work 10 rows in moss st as given for Back.
Change to 4mm (No 8/US 6) needles.
1st row (right side) Moss st 3(5:3), *sl 1 purlwise, k2, moss st, 5(7:9); rep from * to last 6(8:6) sts, sl 1 purlwise, k2, moss st 3(5:3).
2nd row Moss st 3(5:3), *sl 1 purlwise, p2, moss st 5(7:9); rep from * to last 6(8:6) sts, sl 1 purlwise, p2, moss st 3(5:3).
3rd row Moss st 3(5:3), *Tw3, moss st 5(7:9); rep from * to last 6(8:6) sts, Tw3, moss

st 3(5:3).
4th row Moss st 3(5:3), *p3, moss st 5(7:9); rep from * to last 6(8:6) sts, p3, moss st 3(5:3).
These 4 rows form patt. Cont in patt, inc one st at each end of next row and every foll 4th row until there are 65(71:77) sts, working inc sts into patt. Cont straight until Sleeve measures 26(28:31)cm/10¼ (11:12¼)in from beg, ending with a wrong side row. Cast off.

COLLAR
Join right shoulder seam.
With 3¾mm (No 9/US 4) needles and right side facing, k up 16 sts down left front neck, k centre front neck sts, k up 16 sts up right front neck, 5(6:6) sts down

right back neck, k centre back neck sts, k up 6(7:7) sts up left back neck. 83(89:93) sts.
1st rib row P1, [k1, p1] to end.
2nd rib row K1, [p1, k1] to end.
Rep last 2 rows twice more.
Change to 4mm (No 8/US 6) needles.
Work 16 rows in moss st as given for Back. Cast off in moss st.

TO MAKE UP
Join left shoulder and collar seam, reversing seam on moss st section of collar. Wash pieces according to the instructions given on ball band. When dry, sew on sleeves, placing centre of sleeves to shoulder seams. Beginning at top of welts, join side seams, then sleeve seams.

Sailor-collared Jacket page 14

MATERIALS
8(9:10) 50g balls of Rowan Cotton Glace in Navy (A).
Small amount of same in Red, White and Pale Blue.
Pair of 3¼mm (No 10/US 3) knitting needles.
Cable needle.
4(5:5) buttons.

MEASUREMENTS

To fit age	12	24	36 months	
Actual chest	63	66	70	cm
measurement	25	26	27½	in
Length	39	43	49	cm
	15½	17	19¼	in
Sleeve seam	20	22	24	cm
	8	8¾	9½	in

TENSION
25 sts and 34 rows to 10cm/4in square over st st on 3¼mm (No 10/US 3) needles.

ABBREVIATIONS
C4B = sl next 2 sts onto cable needle and leave at back of work, k2, then k2 from cable needle;
C4F = sl next 2 sts onto cable needle and leave at front of work, k2, then k2 from cable needle.
Also see page 40.

LEFT FRONT
With 3¼mm (No 10/US 3) needles and A, cast on 77(79:83) sts.
1st row K1, [p1, k1] to end.
This row forms moss st. Work 5 rows more in moss st, inc one st at centre of last row on **2nd size** only. 77(80:83) sts.
Next row (right side) K to last 4 sts, moss st 4.
Next row Moss st 4, p to end.
Rep last 2 rows until Front measures 13(16:21)cm/5¼(6¼:8¼)in from beg, ending with a right side row.
Dec row Moss st 4, p3(4:5), [p2 tog, p1] twice, [p2 tog] twice, * [p2 tog] 3 times, p3 tog; rep from * 3 times more, [p2 tog] 5 times, [p1, p2 tog] twice, p8(10:12). 46(49:52) sts.
Work in patt as follows:
1st row (right side) K8(10:12), p1, C4B, p1, k19, p1, C4F, p1, k3(4:5), moss st 4.
2nd row Moss st 4, p3(4:5), k1, p4, k1, p19, k1, p4, k1, p8(10:12).
3rd row K8(10:12), p1, k4, p1, k19, p1, k4, p1, k3(4:5), moss st 4.

45

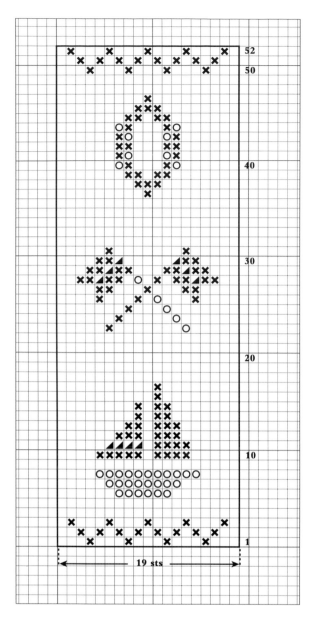

4th row As 2nd row.

These 4 rows form patt. Patt 38 rows.

Shape Armhole

Cast off 3 sts at beg of next row. Work 1 row. Dec one st at armhole edge on next 3 rows. 40(43:46) sts. Patt 11 rows.

Shape Neck

Next row K3(5:7), [k2 tog] twice, k21, [k2 tog] twice, k3(4:5), turn; leave rem 5 sts on a safety pin. 31(34:37) sts. Cont in st st across all sts, dec one st at neck edge on next row and 2(5:8) foll alt rows, then on every 3rd row until 20(21:22) sts rem. Cont straight for a few rows until armhole measures 14(15:16)cm/5½(6:6¼)in, ending at armhole edge.

Shape Shoulder

Cast off 7 sts at beg of next row and foll alt row. Work 1 row. Cast off rem 6(7:8) sts.

Mark front edge to indicate position of 4(5:5) buttons: first one 8(9:10)cm/3¼ (3½:4)in from lower edge, last one 1cm/¼in below neck shaping and rem 2(3:3) evenly spaced between.

RIGHT FRONT

With 3¼mm (No 10/US 3) needles and A, cast on 77(79:83) sts.

Work 6 rows in moss st as given for Left Front, inc one st at centre of last row on **2nd size** only. 77(80:83) sts.

Next row (right side) Moss st 4, k to end.

Next row P to last 4 sts, moss st 4.

Rep last 2 rows until Front measures 8(9:10)cm/3¼(3½:4)in from beg, ending with a wrong side row.

Buttonhole row K1, p1, yrn, p2 tog, patt to end.

Complete as given for Left Front, making buttonholes at markers, reversing shapings and working dec row and patt as follows:

Dec row P8(10:12), [p2 tog, p1] twice, [p2 tog] 5 times, ★ p3 tog, [p2 tog] 3 times; rep from ★ 3 times more, [p2 tog] twice, [p1, p2 tog] twice, p3(4:5), moss st 4. 46(49:52) sts.

1st row (right side) Moss st 4, k3(4:5), p1, C4B, p1, k19, p1, C4F, p1, k8(10:12).

2nd row P8(10:12), k1, p4, k1, p19, k1, p4, k1, p3(4:5), moss st 4.

3rd row Moss st 4, k3(4:5), p1, k4, p1, k19, p1, k4, p1, k8(10:12).

4th row As 2nd row.

BACK

With 3¼mm (No 10/US 3) needles and A, cast on 121(125:129) sts.

Work 6 rows in moss st as given for Left Front.

Beg with a k row, work in st st until Back matches Left Front to armhole shaping, ending with a p row.

Shape Armholes

Cast off 3 sts at beg of next 2 rows. Dec one st at each end of next 3 rows. 109(113:117) sts. Work 1 row.

Dec row K18(20:22), k3 tog, ★[k2 tog] twice, k3 tog; rep from ★ 9 times more, k18(20:22). 67(71:75) sts.

Cont straight until Back matches Left Front to shoulder shaping, ending with a p row.

Sailor-collared Jacket

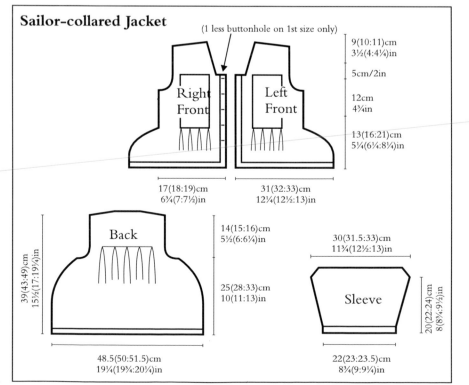

(1 less buttonhole on 1st size only)

Right Front

Left Front

9(10:11)cm
3½(4:4¼)in

5cm/2in

12cm
4¾in

13(16:21)cm
5¼(6¼:8¼)in

17(18:19)cm
6¾(7:7½)in

31(32:33)cm
12¼(12½:13)in

Back

14(15:16)cm
5½(6:6¼)in

30(31.5:33)cm
11¾(12½:13)in

Sleeve

39(43:49)cm
15½(17:19¼)in

25(28:33)cm
10(11:13)in

20(22:24)cm
8(8¾:9½)in

48.5(50:51.5)cm
19¼(19¾:20¼)in

22(23:23.5)cm
8¾(9:9¼)in

Swiss Darning

1. Bring the needle out to the front at the base of the stitch to be covered. Insert the needle under the base of the stitch above. Pull through.

2. Insert the needle back in to the base of the stitch. Emerge at the base of the next stitch to be covered.

MATERIALS
6(6:7) 50g balls of Rowan Cotton Glace.
Pair each of 2¾mm (No 12/US 2) and 3¼mm (No 10/US 3) knitting needles.
4(4:5) buttons.

MEASUREMENTS

To fit age	1	2	3	years
Actual chest	66	72	78	cm
measurement	26	28½	31	in
Length	30	32	34	cm
	11¾	12¾	13½	in
Sleeve seam	21	23	26	cm
	8½	9	10¼	in

TENSION
25 sts and 34 rows to 10cm/4in square over pattern on 3¼mm (No 10/US 3) needles.

ABBREVIATIONS
See page 40.

Shape Shoulders
Cast off 7 sts at beg of next 4 rows and 6(7:8) sts at beg of foll 2 rows.
Cast off rem 27(29:31) sts.

SLEEVES
With 3¼mm (No 10/US 3) needles and A, cast on 43(45:47) sts.
Work 5 rows in moss st as given for Left Front.
Next row Moss st 4(5:6), work twice in next st, [moss st 2, work twice in next st] 11 times, moss st 5(6:7). 55(57:59) sts.
Beg with a k row, work in st st, inc one st at each end of every 5th row until there are 75(79:83) sts. Cont straight until Sleeve measures 20(22:24)cm/8(8¾:9½)in from beg, ending with a p row.
Shape Top
Cast off 3 sts at beg of next 2 rows.
Dec one st at each end of next row and foll alt row. Work 1 row. Cast off rem 65(69:73) sts.

COLLAR
Join shoulder seams.
With 3¼mm (No 10/US 3) needles, rejoin A yarn at inside edge to 5 sts on Right Front safety pin.
Next row K twice in first st, moss st 4.
Next row Moss st 4, p1, p twice in last st.
Next row K twice in first st, k2, moss st 4.
Next row Moss st 4, p3, p twice in last st.
Keeping the 4 sts at outside edge in moss st and remainder in st st as set, inc one st at inside edge on next row and 4(6:8) foll alt rows, then on every 4th row until there

are 19(21:23) sts. Cont straight until inside edge of collar fits up shaped edge of front, ending at inside edge. Leave these sts on a spare needle.
With 3¼mm (No 10/US 3) needles, rejoin A yarn at inside edge to 5 sts on Left Front safety pin.
Next row P twice in first st, moss st 4.
Next row Moss st 4, k1, k twice in last st.
Next row P twice in first st, p2, moss st 4.
Next row Moss st 4, k3, k twice in last st.
Keeping the 4 sts at outside edge in moss st and remainder in st st as set, inc one st at inside edge on next row and 4(6:8) foll alt rows, then on every 4th row until there are 19(21:23) sts. Cont straight until inside edge of collar fits up shaped edge of front, ending at outside edge.
Next row Patt to end, k up 25(27:29) sts across back neck, then patt across sts on spare needle. 63(69:75) sts.
Next row Moss st 4, p to last 4 sts, moss st 4.
Next row Moss st 4, k to last 4 sts, moss st 4.
Rep last 2 rows for a further 13(14:15)cm/5(5½:6)in. Work 6 rows in moss st across all sts. Cast off in moss st.

TO MAKE UP
Swiss darn (see diagram) front motifs between cables, beginning 3 rows above dec row and reversing motifs on one front. Sew front parts of collar in position. Swiss darn buoy motif only on right side of back collar. Join side and sleeve seams. Sew in sleeves. Sew on buttons.

BACK

With 3¼mm (No 10/US 3) needles cast on 84(91:98) sts.
1st to 5th rows Beg with a p row, work 5 rows in st st.
6th row (right side) K2, [k2 tog, yf, k5] to last 5 sts, k2 tog, yf, k3.
7th to 11th rows As 1st to 5th rows.
12th row K5, [k2 tog, yf, k5] to last 2 sts, k2.
These 12 rows form patt. Cont in patt until Back measures 27(29:31)cm/10½ (11¼:12¼)in from beg, ending with a wrong side row.
Shape Shoulders
Cast off 12(13:14) sts at beg of next 2 rows and 13(14:15) sts at beg of foll 2 rows. Cast off rem 34(37:40) sts.

LEFT FRONT

With 3¼mm (No 10/US 3) needles cast on 38(41:45) sts.
1st to 5th rows Beg with a p row, work 5 rows in st st.
6th row [K5, k2 tog, yf] to last 3(6:3) sts, k to end.
7th to 11th rows As 1st to 5th rows.
12th row K2, [k2 tog, yf, k5] to last 1(4:1) sts, [k2 tog, yf] 0(1:0) time, k1(2:1).
These 12 rows form patt. Cont in patt until Front measures 13(14:15)cm/ 5(5½: 6)in from beg, ending with a wrong side row.
Shape Neck
Keeping patt correct, dec one st at neck edge on next row and every foll 3rd row until 25(27:29) sts rem. Cont straight until Front matches Back to shoulder shaping, ending at side edge.
Shape Shoulder
Cast off 12(13:14) sts at beg of next row. Work 1 row. Cast off rem 13(14:15) sts.

RIGHT FRONT

With 3¼mm (No 10/US 3) needles cast on 38(41:45) sts.
1st to 5th rows Beg with a p row, work 5 rows in st st.
6th row K2(5:2), [k2 tog, yf, k5] to last st, k1.
7th to 11th rows As 1st to 5th rows.
12th row K5(2:5), [k2 tog, yf, k5] to last 5(4:5) sts, k2 tog, yf, k3(2:3).
These 12 rows form patt. Complete as Left Front.

SLEEVES

With 3¼mm (No 10/US 3) needles cast on 52(55:59) sts.
1st to 5th rows Beg with a p row, work 5 rows in st st.
6th row K5, [k2 tog, yf, k5] to last 5(1:5) sts, [k2 tog, yf] 1(0:1) time, k3(1:3).
7th to 11th rows Beg with a p row, work 5 rows in st st, inc one st at each end of first row.
12th row Inc in first st, k1, [k2 tog, yf, k5] to last 3(6:3) sts, k2 tog, yf, k0(3:0), inc in last st.

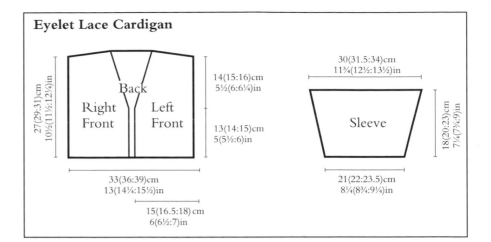

Eyelet Lace Cardigan

These 12 rows set position of patt. Cont in patt, inc one st at each end of every foll 4th(5th:5th) row until there are 76(79:85) sts, working inc sts into patt. Cont straight until Sleeve measures 18(20:23)cm/ 7¼(7¾:9)in from beg, ending with a wrong side row. Cast off.

COLLAR

With 3¼mm (No 10/US 3) needles cast on 70(77:84) sts. Work in patt as given for Back until Collar measures 10(11:12)cm/4(4¼:4¾)in from beg, ending with a wrong side row.
Next row Patt 29(31:33), cast off next 12(15:18) sts, patt to end.
Work on last set of sts only for left side of front collar. Patt 1 row. Keeping patt correct, cast off 3 sts at beg of next row and foll alt row. Dec one st at inside edge on every right side row until 2 sts rem. Work 2 tog and fasten off.
With wrong side facing, rejoin yarn to rem sts and patt to end. Complete as first side.

BUTTON BAND

With 2¾mm (No 12/US 2) needles cast on 8 sts. Work in garter st (every row k) until band, when slightly stretched, fits up straight edge of Left Front to beg of neck shaping. Cast off.
Sew band in place. Mark position of buttons: first one to come 1cm/¼in up from lower edge, last one 2cm/½in below top edge and rem 2(2:3) spaced evenly between.

BUTTONHOLE BAND

Work as given for Button Band making buttonholes to match markers as follows:
Buttonhole row K3, cast off 2, k to end.
Next row K3, cast on 2, k to end.

WELT EDGING

With 2¾mm (No 12/US 2) needles cast on 4 sts. K 1 row.
1st row K2, yf, k2.
2nd row and 2 foll alt rows Sl 1, k to end.
3rd row K3, yf, k2.
5th row K2, yf, k2 tog, yf, k2.
7th row K3, yf, k2 tog, yf, k2.
8th row Cast off 4, k to end.
These 8 rows form patt. Cont in patt until edging, when slightly stretched, fits along lower edge of back and fronts, ending with 8th patt row. Cast off.

CUFF EDGINGS (make 2)

Work as given for Welt Edging until edging, when slightly streched, fits along lower edge of sleeve, ending with 8th patt row. Cast off.

COLLAR EDGING

Work as given for Welt Edging, until edging, when slightly stretched, fits around outside edge of collar, allowing extra for corners and ending with 8th patt row.

TO MAKE UP

Sew on cuff and collar edgings in place. Join shoulder seams. Sew on sleeves, placing centre of sleeve tops to shoulder seams. Join side and sleeve seams. Sew welt edging in place. Sew on buttons and collar, beginning and ending at centre of front bands.

Star Sweater   page 16

MATERIALS
5(6) 50g balls of Rowan DK Handknit
Cotton in Navy (A).
1 ball of same in each of Blue and
White.
Pair each of 3¼mm (No 10/US 3)
and 4mm (No 8/US 6) knitting
needles.
6 buttons.

MEASUREMENTS

To fit age	3-6	6-12	months
Actual chest	59	63	cm
measurement	23½	25	in
Length	31	33	cm
	12¼	13	in
Sleeve seam	17	19	cm
	6¾	7½	in

TENSION
20 sts and 28 rows to 10cm/4in square
over st st on 4mm (No 8/US 6)
needles.

ABBREVIATIONS
See page 40.

NOTES
Read chart from right to left on right
side (k) rows and from left to right on
wrong side (p) rows. When working
motif, use small separate balls of
colours for each coloured area and
twist yarns together on wrong side at
joins to avoid holes.

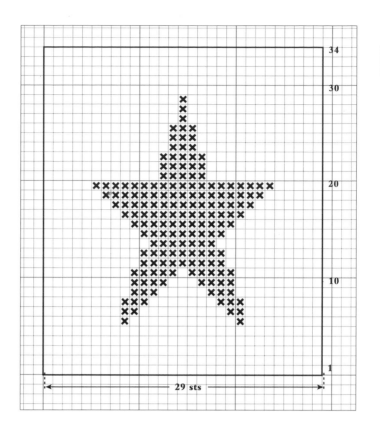

KEY
☐ Blue
☒ White

FRONT
With 3¼mm (No 10/US 3) needles and
A, cast on 59(63) sts.
K 7 rows.
Change to 4mm (No 8/US 6) needles.
Beg with a k row, work 14(20) rows in
st st.
Next row K15(17)A, k across 1st row of
chart, k15(17)A.
Next row P15(17)A, p across 2nd row of
chart, p15(17)A.
Work a further 32 rows as set. Cont in A
only, work 2 rows.
Next row K.
Next row P5, k4, p to last 9 sts, k4, p5.
Rep last 2 rows 7 times more.
Shape Neck
Next row Patt 18(19), turn.

Work on this set of sts only. Patt 3 rows.
Cont in st st until Front measures
30(32)cm/11¾(12½)in from beg, ending
with a p row.
Change to 3¼mm (No 10/US 3) needles.
K 2 rows.
Buttonhole row K4(5), [yf, k2 tog, k5]
twice.
K 3 rows. Cast off.
With right side facing, slip centre 23(25)
sts onto a holder, rejoin yarn and with
4mm (No 8/US 6) needles, patt to end.
Complete as first side, working buttonhole
row as follows:
Buttonhole row [K5, skpo, yf] twice,
k4(5).

BACK
Work as given for Front to neck shaping,
omitting colour motif.
Patt 4 more rows. Cont in st st until Back
measures 27(29)cm/10½(11¼)in from
beg, ending with a p row.
Shape Neck
Next row K18(19), turn.
Work on this set of sts only. Cont until
Back measures 30(32)cm/11¾(12½)in
from beg, ending with a p row.
Change to 3¼mm (No 10/US 3) needles.
K 6 rows. Cast off.
With right side facing, slip centre 23(25)
sts onto a holder, rejoin yarn and with
4mm (No 8/US 6) needles, k to end.
Complete as first side.

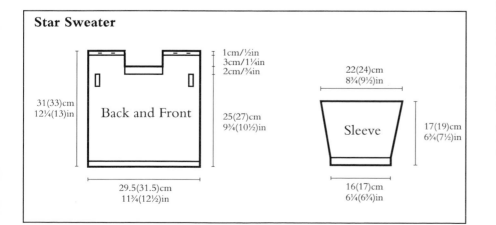

49

SLEEVES

With 3¼mm (No 10/US 3) needles and A, cast on 32(34) sts.
K 5 rows.
Change to 4mm (No 8/US 6) needles. Beg with a k row, work in st st, inc one st at each end of next row and every foll 6th row until there are 44(48) sts. Cont straight until Sleeve measures 17(19)cm/6¾(7½)in from beg. Cast off.

FRONT NECKBAND

With 3¼mm (No 10/US 3) needles, right side facing and A, k up 16 sts down left front neck, k centre front sts, k up 16 sts up right front neck. K 1 row. 55(57) sts.
Buttonhole row K2, yf, k2 tog, k10, skpo, k2 tog, k19(21), skpo, k2 tog, k10, skpo, yf, k2.
K1 row.
Next row K13, skpo, k2 tog, k17(19), skpo, k2 tog, k13.
K 1 row. Cast off, dec at corners as before.

BACK NECKBAND

With 3¼mm (No 10/US 3) needles, right side facing and A, k up 9 sts down right back neck, k centre back sts, k up 9 sts up left back neck. 41(43) sts. K 1 row.
Next row K7, skpo, k2 tog, k19(21), skpo, k2 tog, k7.
K1 row.
Next row K6, skpo, k2 tog, k17(19), skpo, k2 tog, k6.
K 1 row. Cast off, dec at corners as before.

TO MAKE UP

Place buttonhole band over button band on shoulders and catch edges together at sides. Sew on sleeves, placing centre of sleeves in line with buttonholes on shoulders. Join sleeve seams and side seams leaving garter st edge open. Sew on buttons.

MATERIALS

6(7) 50g balls of Rowan DK Handknit Cotton in Black (A).
1 ball of same in each of Red, White and Blue.
Pair each of 3¼mm (No 10/US 3) and 4mm (No 8/US 6) knitting needles.
Set of four 3¼mm (No 10/US 3) double pointed knitting needles.

MEASUREMENTS

To fit age	18-24	24-36	months
Actual chest	75	81	cm
measurement	29½	32	in
Length	38	41	cm
	15	16	in
Sleeve seam	22	24	cm
	8¾	9½	in

TENSION

20 sts and 28 rows to 10cm/4in square over st st on 4mm (No 8/US 6) needles.

ABBREVIATIONS

See page 40.

NOTES

Read chart from right to left on right side (k) rows and from left to right on wrong side (p) rows. When working in pattern from chart, use small separate balls of colours for each coloured area and twist yarns together on wrong side at joins to avoid holes.

FRONT

With 3¼mm (No 10/US 3) needles and A, cast on 74(78) sts.
Beg with a k row, work 4 rows in st st.
1st rib row (right side) K2, [p2, k2] to end.
2nd rib row P2, [k2, p2] to end.
Rib 2 rows more, inc 1(3) sts evenly across last row. 75(81) sts. ★★
Change to 4mm (No 8/US 6) needles. Beg with a k row, work 30(34) rows in st st.
Next row K15(18)A, k across 1st row of chart, k15(18)A.
Next row P15(18)A, p across 2nd row of chart, p15(18)A.
Work a further 42 row as set.
Cont in A only, work 12(16) rows.
Shape Neck
Next row K30(32), turn.
Work on this set of sts only. Dec one st at neck edge on next 6 rows. 24(26) sts.
Work 7 rows straight.
Shape Shoulder
Cast off 12(13) sts at beg of next row. Work 1 row. Cast off rem 12(13) sts.
With right side facing, slip centre 15(17) sts onto a holder, rejoin yarn to rem sts and k to end. Complete as first side, reversing shoulder shaping.

BACK

Work as given for Front to ★★.
Change to 4mm (No 8/US 6) needles. Beg with a k row, work in st st until Back measures same as Front to shoulder shaping, ending with a p row.
Shape Shoulders
Cast off 12(13) sts at beg of next 4 rows. Leave rem 27(29) sts on a spare needle.

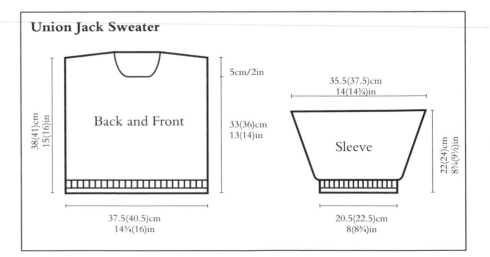

Union Jack Sweater

Back and Front — 38(41)cm 15(16)in — 37.5(40.5)cm 14¾(16)in — 5cm/2in — 33(36)cm 13(14)in

Sleeve — 35.5(37.5)cm 14(14¾)in — 22(24)cm 8¾(9½)in — 20.5(22.5)cm 8(8¾)in

inc in next st] 6 times, rib 1(4). 41(45) sts.
Change to 4mm (No 8/US 6) needles.
Beg with a k row, work in st st, inc one st
at each end of every 3rd row until there
are 71(75) sts. Work 5(9) rows straight.
Cast off.

COLLAR
Join shoulder seams.
With set of four 3¼mm (No 10/US 3)
double pointed needles, A and right side
facing, slip first 7(8) sts from centre front
neck on to safety pin, k rem sts, k up 20
sts up right front neck, k back neck sts inc
one st at centre, k up 20 sts down left
front neck, k sts from safety pin, inc in last
st. 84(88) sts.
1st rib round [K1, p2, k1] to end.
Rib 3 more rounds, turn. Work 14 rows in
rib as set. Cast off in rib.

TO MAKE UP
Sew on sleeves, placing centre of sleeves to
shoulder seams. Join side and sleeve seams,
reversing seam on first and last 4 rows.

SLEEVES
With 3¼mm (No 10/US 3) needles and
A, cast on 34(38) sts.
Beg with a k row, work 4 rows in st st,
then work 9(13) rows in rib as given
for Back.
Next row Rib 2(3), inc in next st, [rib 4,

KEY

☒	Red
☐	White
◣	Blue

44

40

30

20

10

1

45 sts

MATERIALS

15(16) 50g balls of Rowan Denim (see page 40).
Pair each of 3¾mm (No 9/US 4) and 4mm (No 8/US 6) knitting needles.
Cable needle.

MEASUREMENTS

To fit age	3-4	5-6	years

The following measurements are after the garment has been washed according to the instructions given on ball band.

Actual chest	92	100	cm
measurement	36	39½	in
Length	42	46	cm
	16½	18	in
Sleeve seam	25	31	cm
	10	12¼	in

TENSION

20 sts and 28 rows to 10cm/4in square over st st on 4mm (No 8/US 6) needles before washing.

ABBREVIATIONS

C2B = sl next st onto cable needle and leave at back of work, k1, then k1 tbl from cable needle;
C2F = sl next st onto cable needle and leave at front of work, k1 tbl, then k1 from cable needle;
C2BP = sl next st onto cable needle and leave at back of work, p1, then p1 from cable needle;
C2FP = sl next st onto cable needle and leave at front of work, p1, then p1 from cable needle;

Cr2L = sl next st onto cable needle and leave at front of work, p1, then k1 from cable needle;
Cr2R = sl next st onto cable needle and leave at back of work, k1, then p1 from cable needle;
C4B = sl next 2 sts onto cable needle and leave at back of work, k2, then k2 from cable needle;
C4F = sl next 2 sts onto cable needle and leave at front of work, k2, then k2 from cable needle;
Cr4R = sl next 2 sts onto cable needle and leave at back of work, k2, then k1, p1 from cable needle;
Cr4L = sl next 2 sts onto cable needle and leave at front of work, k1 tbl, p1, then k2 from cable needle;
mb = [k1, p1, k1, p1] all in next st, turn, p4, turn, k4, turn, p4, turn, sl 2, k2 tog, pass 2 slipped st over;
Tw4L = sl next 2 sts onto cable needle and leave at front of work, p1, k1, then k2 from cable needle;
Tw4R = sl next 2 sts onto cable needle and leave at back of work, k2, then p1, k1 tbl from cable needle.
Also see page 40.

PANEL A

Worked over 9 sts.
1st row (right side) P2, Cr2R, k1 tbl, Cr2L, p2.
2nd row K2, p1, [k1, p1] twice, k2.
3rd row P1, C2B, p1, k1 tbl, p1, C2F, p1.
4th row K1, p2, k1, p1, k1, p2, k1.
5th row Cr2R, k1 tbl, [p1, k1 tbl] twice, Cr2L.
6th row P1, [k1, p1] 4 times.
7th row Cr2L, k1 tbl, [p1, k1 tbl] twice, Cr2R.
8th row As 4th row.

9th row P1, Cr2L, p1, k1 tbl, p1, Cr2R, p1.
10th row As 2nd row.
11th row P2, Cr2L, k1 tbl, Cr2R, p2.
12th row K3, p3, k3.
13th row P3, sl next 2 sts onto cable needle and leave at back of work, k1, then k1 tbl, k1 from cable needle, p3.
14th row K3, p3, k3.
These 14 rows form patt.

PANEL B

Worked over 5 sts.
1st row (right side) P5.
2nd row K5.
3rd to 6th rows Rep 1st and 2nd rows twice.
7th row P2, mb, p2.
8th row K5.
These 8 rows form patt.

PANEL C

Worked over 12 sts.
1st row (right side) Tw4L, [p1, k1 tbl] 4 times.
2nd row [P1, k1] 4 times, p3, k1.
3rd row Cr2R, Tw4L, [p1, k1 tbl] 3 times.
4th row [P1, k1] 3 times, p3, k2, p1.
5th row Cr2L, Cr2R, Tw4L, [p1, k1 tbl] twice.
6th row [P1, k1] twice, p3, k2, C2FP, k1.
7th row Cr2R, Cr2L, Cr2R, Tw4L, p1, k1 tbl.
8th row P1, k1, p3, k2, C2BP, k2, p1.
9th row [Cr2L, Cr2R] twice, Tw4L.
10th row P3, k2, C2FP, k2, C2FP, k1.
11th row [Cr2R, Cr2L] twice, Tw4R.
12th row As 8th row.
13th row Cr2L, Cr2R, Cr2L, Tw4R, p1, k1 tbl.
14th row As 6th row.
15th row Cr2R, Cr2L, Tw4R, [p1, k1 tbl] twice.
16th row As 4th row.
17th row Cr2L, Tw4R, [p1, k1 tbl] 3 times.

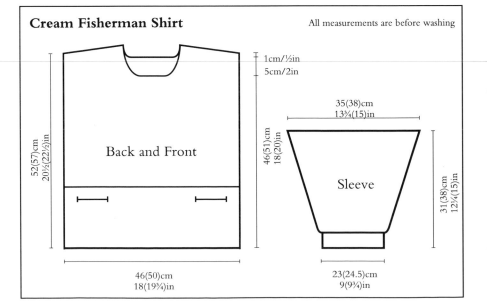

Cream Fisherman Shirt

All measurements are before washing

Back and Front

52(57)cm
20½(22½)in

46(50)cm
18(19¾)in

1cm/½in
5cm/2in

35(38)cm
13¾(15)in

46(51)cm
18(20)in

Sleeve

31(38)cm
12¼(15)in

23(24.5)cm
9(9¾)in

18th row As 2nd row.
19th row Tw4R, [p1, k1 tbl] 4 times.
20th row [P1, k1] 5 times, p2.
These 20 rows form patt.

PANEL D
Worked over 41 sts.
1st row (right side) P8, *[Cr2R] twice, p1, [Cr2L] twice, p7; rep from * once more, p1.
2nd row K8, *p1 tbl, k1, p1 tbl, k3, p1 tbl, k1, p1 tbl, k7; rep from * once more, k1.
3rd row P7, *[Cr2R] twice, p3, [Cr2L] twice, p5; rep from * once more, p2.
4th row K7, *p1 tbl, k1, p1 tbl, k5; rep from * 3 times more, k2.
5th row P6, *[Cr2R] twice, p5, [Cr2L] twice, p3; rep from * once more, p3.
6th row K6, *p1 tbl, k1, p1 tbl, k7, p1 tbl, k1, p1 tbl, k3; rep from * once more, k3.
7th row P5, *[Cr2R] twice, p7, [Cr2L] twice, p1; rep from * once more, p4.
8th row K5, *p1 tbl, k1, p1 tbl, k9, [p1 tbl, k1] twice; rep from * once more, k4.
9th row P4, mb, *k1, p1, k1, p9, k1, p1, k1, mb; rep from * once more, p4.
10th row As 8th row.
11th row P5, *[Cr2L] twice, p7, [Cr2R] twice, p1; rep from * once more, p4.
12th row As 6th row.
13th row P6, *[Cr2L] twice, p5, [Cr2R] twice, p3; rep from * once more, p3.
14th row As 4th row.
15th row P7, *[Cr2L] twice, p3, [Cr2R] twice, p5; rep from * once more, p2.
16th row As 2nd row.
17th row P8, *[Cr2L] twice, p1, [Cr2R] twice, p7; rep from * once more, p1.
18th row K9, *p1 tbl, [k1, p1 tbl] 3 times, k9; rep from * once more.
19th row P9, *k1, p1, k1, mb, k1, p1, k1, p9; rep from * once more.
20th row As 18th row.
These 20 rows form patt.

PANEL E
Worked over 12 sts.
1st row (right side) [K1 tbl, p1] 4 times, Cr4R.
2nd row K1, p3, [k1, p1] 4 times.
3rd row [K1 tbl, p1] 3 times, Cr4R, Cr2L.
4th row P1, k2, p3, [k1, p1] 3 times.
5th row [K1 tbl, p1] twice, Cr4R, Cr2L, Cr2R.
6th row K1, C2BP, k2, p3, [k1, p1] twice.
7th row K1 tbl, p1, Cr4R, Cr2L, Cr2R, Cr2L.
8th row P1, k2, C2FP, k2, p3, k1, p1.
9th row Cr4R, [Cr2L, Cr2R] twice.
10th row K1, C2BP, k2, C2BP, k2, p3.
11th row Cr4L, [Cr2R, Cr2L] twice.
12th row As 8th row.
13th row K1 tbl, p1, Cr4L, Cr2R, Cr2L, Cr2R.
14th row As 6th row.
15th row [K1 tbl, p1] twice, Cr4L, Cr2R, Cr2L.
16th row As 4th row.
17th row [K1 tbl, p1] 3 times, Cr4L, Cr2R.
18th row As 2nd row.
19th row [K1 tbl, p1] 4 times, Cr4L.
20th row P2, [k1, p1] 5 times.
These 20 rows form patt.

BACK
With 3¾mm (No 9/US 4) needles cast on 111(123) sts.
1st row (right side) K3, *p2, Cr2R, k1, Cr2L, p2, k3; rep from * to end.
2nd row P3, *k2, p1, [k1, p1] twice, k2, p3; rep from * to end.
3rd row K3, *p1, Cr2R, p1, k1, p1, Cr2L, p1, k3; rep from * to end.
4th row P3, *k1, p1, [k2, p1] twice, k1, p3; rep from * to end.
5th row K3, *Cr2R, p2, k1, p2, Cr2L, k3; rep from * to end.
6th row P3, *k4, p1, k4, p3; rep from * to end.
These 6 rows form welt patt. **Rep last 6 rows 7(8) times more. ***K 4 rows, inc 10 sts evenly across last row. 121(133) sts. Change to 4mm (No 8/US 6) needles.
1st row (right side) P2, [k4, p2] 1(2) times, work 1st row of panel A, panel B and panel C, p2, k4, work 1st row of panel D, k4, p2, work 1st row of panel E, panel B and panel A, [p2, k4] 1(2) times, p2.
2nd row K2, [p4, k2] 1(2) times, work 2nd row of panel A, panel B and panel E, k2, p4, work 2nd row of panel D, p4, k2, work 2nd row of panel C, panel B and panel A, [k2, p4] 1(2) times, k2.
3rd row P2, [C4F, p2] 1(2) times, work 3rd row of panel A, panel B and panel C, p2, C4F, work 3rd row of panel D, C4B, p2, work 3rd row of panel E, panel B and panel A, [p2, C4B] 1(2) times, p2.
4th row K2, [p4, k2] 1(2) times, work 4th row of panel A, panel B and panel E, k2, p4, work 4th row of panel D, p4, k2, work 4th row of panel C, panel B and panel A, [k2, p4] 1(2) times, k2.
These 4 rows set position of panels and form cable patt between panels.*** Patt a further 90(100) rows.
Shape Neck
Next row Patt 47(51), turn.
Work on this set of sts only. Keeping patt correct, cast off 3 sts at beg of next row and foll alt row. 41(45) sts.
Shape Shoulder
Cast off 14(15) sts at beg of next row and foll alt row. Work 1 row. Cast off rem 13(15) sts.
With right side facing, slip centre 27(31) sts onto a holder, rejoin yarn to rem sts, patt to end. Patt 1 row. Complete to match first side.

POCKET LININGS (MAKE 2)
With 4mm (No 8/US 6) needles cast on 24 sts.
Beg with a k row, work 30 rows in st st, inc 3 sts evenly across last row. 27 sts.
Leave these sts on a holder.

FRONT
Work as given for Back to **. Rep last 6 rows 4(5) times more, then work 1st to 5th row.
Place Pockets
Next row Patt 12, cast off next 27 sts, patt to last 39 sts, cast off next 27 sts, patt to end.
Next row Patt 12, patt across sts of first pocket lining, patt to last 12 sts, patt across sts of second pocket lining, patt to end.

Welt patt 11 rows more. Work as given for Back from *** to ***.
Patt a further 76(86) rows.
Shape Neck
Next row Patt 49(53), turn.
Work on this set of sts only. Dec one st at neck edge on next 8 rows. 41(45) sts. Patt 9 rows straight.
Shape Shoulder
Cast off 14(15) sts at beg of next row and foll alt row. Work 1 row. Cast off rem 13(15) sts.
With right side facing, slip centre 23(27) sts onto a holder, rejoin yarn to rem sts, patt to end. Complete to match first side.

SLEEVES
With 3¾mm (No 9/US 4) needles cast on 59 sts.
1st row (right side) K1, p2, Cr2R, k1, Cr2L, p2, *k3, p2, Cr2R, k1, Cr2L, p2; rep from * to last st, k1.
2nd row P1, k2, p1, [k1, p1] twice, k2, *p3, k2, p1, [k1, p1] twice, k2; rep from * to last st, p1.
These 2 rows set welt patt. Welt patt a further 16 rows, inc 2(6) sts evenly across last row. 61(65) sts.
Change to 4mm (No 8/US 6) needles.
1st row (right side) P0(1), k0(1) tbl, Cr2L, p4, k4, work 1st row of panel D k4, p4, Cr2R, k0(1) tbl, p0(1).
2nd row [K1, p1] 1(2) times, k4, p4, work 2nd row of panel D, p4, k4, [p1, k1] 1(2) times.
These 2 rows set position of panels and cable pattern between panels. Cont in patt, inc one st at each end of 3rd row and every foll 5th row until there are 85(93) sts, working inc sts into panel A and panel B patt then into reverse st st. Patt 10(20) rows straight. Cast off.

NECKBAND
Join right shoulder seam.
With 3¾mm (No 9/US 4) needles and right side facing, k up 17(18) sts down left front neck, k centre front sts, k up 17(18) sts up right front neck, k up 7(8) sts down right back neck, k centre back sts, k up 8(9) sts up left back neck. 99(111) sts.
1st rib row K3, [p3, k3] to end.
2nd rib row P3, [k3, p3] to end.
Rep last 2 rows 5 times more.
Change to 4mm (No 8/US 6) needles.
Beg with a 1st row, work 18 rows in welt patt as given for Back. Cast off loosely in patt.

TO MAKE UP
Join left shoulder and neckband seam, reversing seam on last 18 rows of neckband. Catch down pocket linings on wrong side. Wash pieces according to instructions given on ball band. When dry, sew on sleeves, placing centre of sleeves to shoulder seams. Join side and sleeve seams.

MATERIALS

13 50g balls of Rowan DK Handknit Cotton.
Pair each of 3¼mm (No 10/US 3) and 4mm (No 8/US 6) knitting needles.
One 3¼mm (No 10/US 3) circular knitting needle.
Cable needle.
5 buttons.

MEASUREMENTS

To fit age	4-6	years
Actual chest	94	cm
measurement	37	in
Length	54	cm
	21¼	in
Sleeve seam	30	cm
	11¾	in

TENSION

20 sts and 28 rows to 10cm/4in square over st st on 4mm (No 8/US 6) needles.

ABBREVIATIONS

C3F = sl next 2 sts onto cable needle and leave at front of work, k1 tbl, then k2 from cable needle;
C3B = sl next st onto cable needle and leave at back of work, k2, then k1 tbl from cable needle;
C4B = sl next 2 sts onto cable needle and leave at back of work, k2, then k2 from cable needle;
C4F = sl next 2 sts onto cable needle and leave at front of work, k2, then k2 from cable needle;
Cr3L = sl next 2 sts onto cable needle and leave at front of work, p1, then k2 from cable needle;
Cr3R = sl next st onto cable needle and leave at back of work, k2, then p1 from cable needle;
Tw4R = sl next 2 sts onto cable needle and leave at back of work, k2, then k1 tbl, p1 from cable needle;
Tw4L = sl next 2 sts onto cable needle and leave at front of work, p1, k1 tbl, then k2 from cable needle.
Also see page 40.

PANEL A

Worked over 7 sts.
1st row (right side) K5, p1, k1.
2nd row P2, k1, p4.
3rd row K3, [p1, k1] twice.
4th row P2, k1, p1, k1, p2.
5th row K1, [p1, k1] 3 times.
6th row As 4th row.
7th row As 3rd row.

8th row As 2nd row.
9th row As 1st row.
10th row P7.
These 10 rows form patt.

PANEL B

Worked over 12 sts.
1st row (right side) P2, k4, [p1, k1] twice, p2.
2nd row K3, p1, k1, p5, k2.
3rd and 4th rows As 1st and 2nd rows.
5th row P2, sl next 4 sts onto cable needle and leave at back of work, [p1, k1] twice, then k4 from cable needle, p2.
6th row K2, p4, [k1, p1] twice, k2.
7th row P3, k1, p1, k5, p2.
8th to 13th rows Rep 6th and 7th rows 3 times.
14th row As 6th row.
15th row P2, sl next 4 sts onto cable needle and leave at back of work, k4, then [p1, k1] twice from cable needle, p2.
16th row As 2nd row.
17th to 20th rows Rep 1st and 2nd rows twice.
These 20 rows form patt.

PANEL C

Worked over 7 sts.
1st row (right side) K1, p1, k5.
2nd row P4, k1, p2.
3rd row [K1, p1] twice, k3.
4th row P2, k1, p1, k1, p2.
5th row K1, [p1, k1] 3 times.
6th row As 4th row.
7th row As 3rd row.
8th row As 2nd row.
9th row As 1st row.
10th row P7.
These 10 rows form patt.

PANEL D

Worked over 19 sts.
1st row (right side) P2, k3, [p1, k1] 3 times, k4, p4.
2nd row K4, p4, [k1, p1] 3 times, k1, p2, k2.

3rd row P2, Cr3L, [p1, k1] 3 times, C4F, p4.
4th row K4, p4, [k1, p1] 3 times, p2, k3.
5th row P3, Cr3L, k1, p1, k1, Tw4R, C3F, p3.
6th row K3, p2, p1 tbl, k1, p1 tbl, p2, k1, p1, k1, p2, k4.
7th row P4, Cr3L, Tw4R, k1 tbl, p1, k1 tbl, Cr3L, p2.
8th row K2, p2, [k1, p1 tbl] 3 times, p4, k5.
9th row P5, Tw4R, [k1 tbl, p1] 3 times, k2, p2.
10th row K2, p2, [k1, p1 tbl] 4 times, p2, k5.
11th row P3, Tw4R, [k1 tbl, p1] 3 times, k1 tbl, Cr3R, p2.
12th row K3, p2, [p1 tbl, k1] 4 times, p1 tbl, p2, k3.
13th row P2, Cr3R, [k1 tbl, p1] 3 times, k1 tbl, sl next 2 sts onto cable needle and leave at back of work, k2, then p2 from cable needle, p3.
14th row K5, p2, [p1 tbl, k1] 4 times, p2, k2.
15th row P2, k2, [p1 k1 tbl] 3 times, C4B, p5.
16th row K5, p4, [p1 tbl, k1] 3 times, p2, k2.
17th row P2, Cr3L, k1 tbl, p1, k1 tbl, Tw4R, C3F, p4.
18th row K4, p2, k1, p1, k1, p2, p1 tbl, k1, p1 tbl, p2, k3.
19th row P3, Cr3L, Tw4R, k1, p1, k1, Cr3L, p3.
20th row K3, p2, [k1, p1] 3 times, p4, k4.
21st row P4, C4F, [k1, p1] 3 times, C3F, p2.
22nd row K2, p2, k1, [p1, k1] 3 times, p4, k4.
23rd row P4, k5, [p1, k1] 3 times, k2, p2.
24th row As 22nd row.
25th row P4, C4F, [k1, p1] 3 times, Cr3R, p2.
26th row As 20th row.
27th row P3, C3B, Tw4L, k1, p1, k1, Cr3R, p3.
28th row As 18th row.

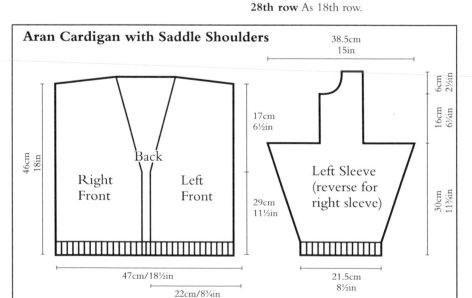

Aran Cardigan with Saddle Shoulders

38.5cm
15in

46cm
18in

Back

Right Front

Left Front

47cm/18½in

22cm/8¾in

17cm
6½in

29cm
11½in

6cm
2½in

16cm
6¼in

30cm
11¾in

Left Sleeve (reverse for right sleeve)

21.5cm
8½in

29th row P2, Cr3R, k1 tbl, p1, k1 tbl, Tw4L, Cr3R, p4.
30th row As 16th row.
31st row P2, k2, [p1, k1 tbl] 3 times, Tw4L, p5.
32nd row As 14th row.
33rd row P2, Cr3L, k1 tbl, [p1, k1 tbl] 3 times, Tw4L, p3.
34th row As 12th row.
35th row P3, sl next 2 sts onto cable needle and leave at front of work, p2, then k2 from cable needle, k1 tbl, [p1, k1 tbl] 3 times, Cr3L, p2.
36th row As 10th row.
37th row P5, C4F, [k1 tbl, p1] 3 times, k2, p2.
38th row As 8th row.
39th row P4, C3B, Tw4L, k1 tbl, p1, k1 tbl, Cr3R, p2.
40th row As 6th row.
41st row P3, Cr3R, k1, p1, k1, Tw4L, Cr3R, p3.
42nd row As 4th row.
43rd row P2, C3B, [p1, k1] 3 times, C4F, p4.
44th row As 2nd row.
These 44 rows form patt.

BACK
With 3¼mm (No 10/US 3) needles cast on 120 sts.
1st rib row *P2, [k2, p2] twice, k4*; rep from * to * twice more, p2, [k2, p2] 3 times, k4, rep from * to * twice, p2, [k2, p2] 3 times, k4, p2, [k2, p2] 3 times.
2nd rib row K2, [p2, k2] 3 times, p4, k2, [p2, k2] 3 times, *p4, k2, [p2, k2] twice*; rep from * to * once more, p4, k2, [p2, k2] 3 times, rep from * to * 3 times.
3rd rib row *P2, [k2, p2] twice, C4F*; rep from * to * twice more, p2, [k2, p2] 3 times, C4F, rep from * to * twice, p2, [k2, p2] 3 times, C4F, p2, [k2, p2] 3 times.
4th rib row As 2nd rib row.
Rib 11 rows more.
Next row Rib 24, p2 tog, rib 13, m1, rib 8, p2 tog, rib 21, p2 tog, rib 13, m1, rib 8, p2 tog, rib to end. 118 sts.
Change to 4mm (No 8/US 6) needles.
1st row (right side) K1, [work 1st row of panel A, panel B, panel C and panel D] twice, work 1st row of panel A, panel B and panel C, k1.
2nd row P1, [work 2nd row of panel C, panel B, panel A and panel D] twice, work 2nd row of panel C, panel B and panel A, p1.
These 2 rows set position of panels. Cont in patt until Back measures 46cm/18in from beg, ending with a wrong side row.
Shape Shoulders
Cast off 20 sts at beg of next 4 rows. Cast off rem 38 sts.

LEFT FRONT
With 3¼mm (No 10/US 3) needles cast on 55 sts.
1st rib row *P2, [k2, p2] twice, k4; rep from * twice more, [p2, k2] 3 times, k1.
2nd rib row P3, *k2, [p2, k2] twice, p4; rep from * twice more, k2, [p2, k2] twice.
3rd rib row *P2, [k2, p2] twice, C4F; rep from * twice more, [p2, k2] 3 times, k1.
4th rib row As 2nd rib row.
Rib 11 rows more.

Next row Rib 5, p2 tog, rib 13, m1, rib 8, p2 tog, rib to end. 54 sts.
Change to 4mm (No 8/US 6) needles.
1st row (right side) K1, work 1st row of panel A, panel B, panel C, panel D and panel A, k1.
2nd row P1, work 2nd row of panel A, panel D, panel C, panel B and panel A, p1.
These 2 rows set position of panels. Cont in patt until Front measures 29cm/11½in from beg, ending with a wrong side row.
Shape Neck
Keeping patt correct, dec one st at end of next row and at same edge on every foll 3rd row until 40 sts rem.
Cont straight until Front matches Back to shoulder shaping, ending with a wrong side row.
Shape Shoulder
Cast off 20 sts at beg of next row. Work 1 row. Cast off rem 20 sts.

RIGHT FRONT
With 3¼mm (No 10/US 3) needles cast on 55 sts.
1st rib row (right side) K3, p2, k4, p2, [k2, p2] twice, *k4, p2, [k2, p2] 3 times; rep from * once more.
2nd rib row *K2, [p2, k2] 3 times, p4; rep from * once more, k2, [p2, k2] twice, p4, k2, p3.
3rd row K3, p2, C4F, p2, [k2, p2] twice, *C4F, p2, [k2, p2] 3 times; rep from * once more.
4th row As 2nd row.
Rib 11 rows more.
Next row Rib 24, p2 tog, rib 13, m1, rib 8, p2 tog, rib 6. 54 sts.
Change to 4mm (No 8/US 6) needles.
1st row (right side) K1, work 1st row of panel C, panel D, panel A, panel B and panel C, k1.
2nd row P1, work 2nd row of panel C, panel B, panel A, panel D and panel C, p1.
Complete as given for Left Front, reversing shapings.

LEFT SLEEVE
With 3¼mm (No 10/US 3) needles cast on 46 sts.

1st rib row (right side) K2, [p2, k2] to end.
2nd rib row P2, [k2, p2] to end.
Rib 13 rows.
Next row Rib 1, [m1, rib 2] 4 times, rib 2, m1, rib 14, m1, rib 10, m1, rib 4, [m1, rib 2] 3 times, m1, rib 1. 57 sts.
Change to 4mm (No 8/US 6) needles.
1st row (right side) Work 1st row of panel B, panel C, panel D, panel A and panel B.
2nd row Work 2nd row of panel B, panel A, panel D, panel C and panel B.
These 2 rows set position of panels. Cont in patt, inc one st at each end of next row and 3 foll 2nd rows, then on every foll 4th row until there are 91 sts, working inc sts into patt of panel A at left edge and panel C at right edge, then into reverse st st. Cont straight until Sleeve measures 30cm/11¾in from beg, ending with a wrong side row.
Shape Saddle
Cast off 28 sts at beg of next 2 rows. Work straight on rem 35 sts for a further 16cm/6¼in, ending with a wrong side row. ★★
Shape Neck
Next row Patt 16, work 2 tog and turn; leave rem 17 sts on a holder.
Dec one st at inside edge on next 6 rows. 11 sts. Work straight until saddle measures 22cm/8¾in, ending with a wrong side row. Cast off.

RIGHT SLEEVE
Work as given for Left Sleeve to ★★.
Shape Neck
Next row Patt 17 and sl these sts onto a holder; work 2 tog, patt to end.
Complete as given for Left Sleeve.

FRONT BANDS AND COLLAR
Sew saddles to front and back, then join seam at centre back.
With 3¼mm (No 10/US 3) circular needle and right side facing, k up 69 sts along straight edge of right front, 50 sts along shaped edge to shoulder, k sts of right sleeve saddle, dec 4 sts, k up 7 sts along shaped edge of saddle, 24 sts along back neck, 7 sts along shaped edge of left sleeve saddle, k sts from left saddle, dec 4 sts, k up 50 sts along shaped edge of left front and 69 sts along straight edge. 302 sts.
Work backwards and forwards in rows. Work 2nd row of rib as given for Left Sleeve.
Next 2 rows Rib to last 75 sts, turn.
Next 2 rows Rib to last 81 sts, turn.
Next 2 rows Rib to last 87 sts, turn.
Cont in this way, working 6 sts less at end of next 12 rows, turn, rib to end.
Rib 1 row across all sts.
Buttonhole row Rib 3, [cast off 2, rib 12 sts more] 5 times, rib to end.
Next row Rib to end, casting on 2 sts over those cast off in previous row.
Rib 4 rows. Cast off in rib.

TO MAKE UP
Sew remainder of sleeve tops in place. Join side and sleeve seams. Sew on buttons.

Multicoloured Sweater   page 22

MATERIALS

3(3:4) 50g balls of Rowan DK
Handknit Cotton in Navy (A).
2(2:3) balls of same in Red (B).
1(1:2) balls of same in each of Gold
(C) and Mid Blue (D).
1 ball of same in each of Lime (E) and
Light Blue (F).
Small amount of same in Cream (G).
Pair each of 3¼mm (No 10/US 3)
and 4mm (No 8/US 6) knitting
needles.

MEASUREMENTS

To fit age	2-3	3-4	4-5 years
Actual chest	78	84	90	cm
measurement	30½	33	35½	in
Length	40	43	46	cm
	15¾	17	18	in
Sleeve seam	25	28	34	cm
	10	11	13½	in

TENSION

20 sts and 28 rows to 10cm/4in square
over st st on 4mm (No 8/US 6)
needles.

ABBREVIATIONS

See page 40.

BACK

With 3¼mm (No 10/US 3) needles and
E, cast on 78(82:90) sts.
K 1 row. Change to A and beg with a p
row, work 3 rows in st st.
1st rib row (right side) K2, [p2, k2]
to end.
2nd rib row P2, [k2, p2] to end.
Rep last 2 rows twice, inc 2 sts evenly
across last row on **2nd size** only.
78(84:90) sts.
Change to 4mm (No 8/US 6) needles.
Beg with a k row, work 6 rows in st st.
Cont in st st and stripe patt of 4 rows B, 2
rows C, 4 rows B, 1 row A, 3 rows D, 1
row E, 3 rows D, 4 rows A, 1 row G, 2
rows C, 2 rows B, 4 rows F, 5 rows A, 2
rows E, 2 rows A until Back measures
40(43:46)cm/15¾(17:18)in from beg,
ending with a p row.

Shape Shoulders

Cast off 12(13:14) sts at beg of next 4
rows. Leave rem 30(32:34) sts on a holder.

FRONT

Work as given for Back until Front
measures 32(33:34)cm/12½(13:13¼)in
from beg, ending with a p row.

Shape Neck

Next row K38(41:44), turn.
Work on this set of sts only. Dec one st at
neck edge on every row until 24(26:28)
sts rem. Cont straight until Front matches
Back to shoulder shaping, ending at
side edge.

Shape Shoulder

Cast off 12(13:14) sts at beg of next row.
Work 1 row. Cast off rem 12(13:14) sts.
With right side facing, sl centre 2 sts onto
a safety pin, rejoin yarn to rem sts and k
to end. Complete as given for first side.

SLEEVES

With 3¼mm (No 10/US 3) needles and
E, cast on 38(38:42) sts.
K 1 row. Change to A and beg with a p
row, work 3 rows in st st. Now work 12
rows in rib as given for Back welt, inc
6(8:6) sts evenly across last row.
44(46:48) sts.
Change to 4mm (No 8/US 6) needles.
Beg with a k row, work 6 rows in st st, inc
one st at each end of 5th row. Cont in st st
and stripe patt as given for Back, inc one
st at each end of 3rd(4th:5th) row and
every foll 4th(5th:6th) row until there are
64(68:72) sts. Cont straight until Sleeve
measures 25(28:34)cm/10(11:13½)in from
beg, ending with a p row. Cast off.

NECKBAND

Join right shoulder seam.
With 3¼mm (No 10/US 3) needles, right
side facing and A, k up 34(38:42) sts down
left front neck, k 2 sts from safety pin
(mark these 2 sts), k up 34(36:42) sts up
right front neck, k back neck sts.
100(108:120) sts.
1st rib row P2, [k2, p2] to 2 sts before
marked sts, k2 tog tbl, p2, k2tog, [p2, k2]
to end.
2nd rib row P2, [k2, p2] to 3 sts before
marked sts, k1, k2 tog tbl, k2, k2 tog, k1,
[p2, k2] to end.
3rd row Rib to 2 sts before marked sts,
p2 tog tbl, p2, p2 tog, rib to end.
4th row Rib to 2 sts before marked sts,
p2 tog tbl, k2, p2 tog, rib to end.
5th row With E, rib to 2 sts before
marked sts, k2 tog tbl, p2, k2 tog, rib to
end.
With E, cast off in rib, dec at centre front
as before.

TO MAKE UP

Join left shoulder and neckband seam. Sew
on sleeves, placing centre of sleeves to
shoulder seams. Join side and sleeve seams,
reversing seam on first and last 4 rows.

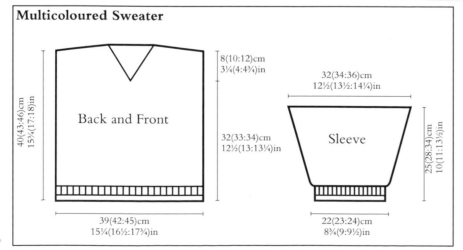

Multicoloured Sweater

Back and Front

40(43:46)cm
15¾(17:18)in

8(10:12)cm
3¼(4:4¾)in

32(33:34)cm
12½(13:13¼)in

39(42:45)cm
15¼(16½:17¾)in

Sleeve

32(34:36)cm
12½(13½:14¼)in

25(28:34)cm
10(11:13½)in

22(23:24)cm
8¾(9:9½)in

Tartan and Boats Cardigan page 23

MATERIALS
5(7) 50g balls of Rowan DK Handknit Cotton in Cream (A).
2 balls of same in each of Blue (B) and Green (C).
1 ball of same in each of Red (D) and Yellow (E).
Pair each of 3¼mm (No 10/US 3) and 4mm (No 8/US 6) knitting needles.
One 3¼mm (No 10/US 3) circular knitting needle.
4 buttons.

MEASUREMENTS

To fit age	2-3	4-6	years
Actual chest	80	91	cm
measurement	31½	36	in
Length	35	39	cm
	13¾	15½	in
Sleeve seam	27	31	cm
	10¾	12¼	in

TENSION
21 sts and 25 rows to 10cm/4in square over tartan pattern on 4mm (No 8/US 6) needles.

ABBREVIATIONS
See page 40.

NOTES
Read charts from right to left on right side (k) rows and from left to right on wrong side (p) rows. When working two colour rib, strand yarn when not in use loosely across wrong side to keep fabric elastic. When working boat motifs or tartan pattern, use separate small balls of contrast colours for each coloured area and twist yarns together on wrong side at joins to avoid holes.

BACK AND FRONTS
Knitted in one piece to armholes.
With 3¼mm (No 10/US 3) needles and B, cast on 160(180) sts.
K 1 row. With A, p 1 row. With D, k 1 row. With A, p 1 row.
1st rib row (right side) K3C, [p2A, k2C] to last st, k1C.
2nd rib row P3C, [k2A, p2C] to last st, p1C.
3rd and 4th rows With E, work 1st and 2nd rows.
5th and 6th rows As 1st and 2nd rows.
Change to 4mm (No 8/US 6) needles. With A, k 1 row, inc 1(5) sts across. 161(185) sts. With D, p 1 row. Cont in st st and work 1st to 15th rows of chart 1. Now work in patt from chart 2 until work measures 18(20)cm/7(8)in from beg, ending with a wrong side row.
Right Front
Next row Patt 40(45), turn.
Work on this set of sts only. Patt 5 rows. Dec one st at beg of next row and every foll alt row until 26(31) sts rem. Cont straight until Front measures 35(39)cm/13¾(15½)in from beg, ending with a right side row.
Shape Shoulder
Cast off 13(15) sts at beg of next row.
Work 1 row. Cast off rem 13(16) sts.
Back
With right side facing, rejoin yarn to rem sts, patt 81(95) sts, turn. Work on this set of sts only until Back measures same as Right Front to shoulder shaping, ending with a wrong side row.

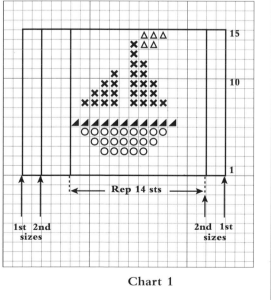

Chart 1

KEY

- ☐ Cream (A)
- ✖ Blue (B)
- ◯ Green (C)
- △ Red (D)
- ◢ Yellow (E)

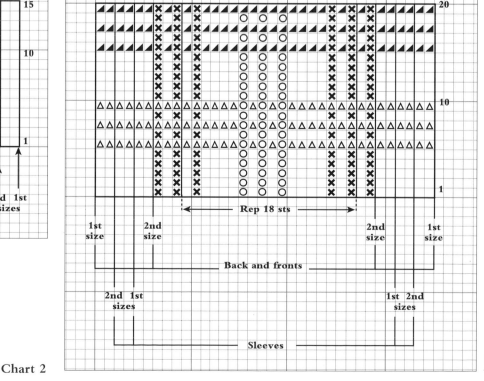

Chart 2

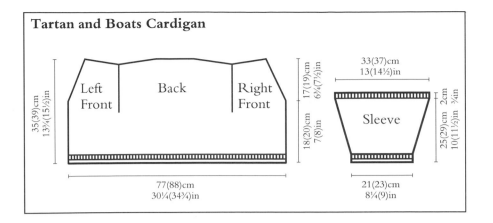

Tartan and Boats Cardigan

Left Front — **Back** — **Right Front**

35(39)cm
13¾(15½)in

17(19)cm
6¾(7½)in

18(20)cm
7(8)in

77(88)cm
30¼(34¾)in

Sleeve

33(37)cm
13(14½)in

2cm
¾in

25(29)cm
10(11½)in

21(23)cm
8¼(9)in

Shape Shoulders
Cast off 13(15) sts at beg of next 2 rows and 13(16) sts at beg of foll 2 rows. Leave rem 29(33) sts on a holder.

Left Front
With right side facing, rejoin yarn to rem sts and patt to end. Complete to match Right Front.

SLEEVES
With 3¼mm (No 10/US 3) needles and B, cast on 38(42) sts. K 1 row. With A, p 1 row. With D, k 1 row. With A, p1 row.

1st rib row (right side) K2C, [p2A, k2C] to end.
2nd rib row P2C, [k2A, p2C] to end.
3rd and 4th rows With E, work 1st and 2nd rows.
5th and 6th rows As 1st and 2nd rows, inc 7 sts evenly across last row. 45(49) sts. Change to 4mm (No 8/US 6) needles. Beg with a k row and 1st(11th) row of chart, work in st st and patt from chart 2, inc one st at each end of 3rd row and every foll 4th row until there are 69(77) sts, working inc sts into patt. Cont straight

until Sleeve measures 25(29)cm/10(11½)in from beg, ending with a wrong side row and inc one st at centre of last row. 70(78) sts. Now work the 6 rows of rib as given for cuff. Cast off in rib.

FRONT BAND
Join shoulder seams.
With 3¼mm (No 10/US 3) circular needle, right side facing and A, k up 44(48) sts up straight front edge of right front, omitting rolled up edge, 40(44) sts up shaped edge to shoulder, k back neck sts inc one st, k up 40(44) sts down shaped edge of left front to beg of neck shaping and 44(48) sts along straight edge, omitting rolled up edge. 198(218) sts. Work backwards and forwards.
1st rib row P2C, [k2A, p2C] to end.
2nd rib row K2C, [p2A, k2C] to end.
3rd row With E, work 1st row.
Buttonhole row With E, rib 4, [yon, k2 tog, rib 10] 4 times, rib to end.
Rep 1st and 2nd rows. With A, p 1 row. With D, k1 row. With A, p 1 row. With B, k 1 row. With B, cast off purlwise.

TO MAKE UP
Sew in sleeves. Join sleeve seams. Sew on buttons.

Lace Fisher Jersey   page 25

MATERIALS
9(10) 50g balls of Rowan Cotton Glace.
Pair each of 3mm (No 11/US 2) and 3¼mm (No 10/US 3) knitting needles.
Set of four 3mm (No 11/US 2) double pointed knitting needles.
Cable needle.

MEASUREMENTS

To fit age	2-3	4-6	years
Actual chest	80	87	cm
measurement	31½	34	in
Length	44	48	cm
	17¼	19	in
Sleeve seam	25	30	cm
	10	12	in

TENSION
25 sts and 34 rows to 10cm/4in square over st st on 3¼mm (No 10/US 3) needles.

ABBREVIATIONS
mb = [k1, p1, k1, p1, k1] all in next st, turn, p5, pass 2nd, 3rd, 4th and 5th st over first st, turn, k1 tbl.
Also see page 40.

PANEL A
Worked over 11(13) sts.
1st row (right side) K5(6), p1, k5(6).
2nd row P4(5), k1, p1, k1, p4(5).
3rd row K3(4), p1, [k1, p1] twice, k3(4).
4th row P2(3), k1, [p1, k1] 3 times, p2(3).
5th row K1(2), p1, [k1, p1] 4 times, k1(2).
6th row As 4th row.
7th row As 3rd row.
8th row As 2nd row.
9th row As 1st row.
10th row P11(13).
These 10 rows form patt.

PANEL B
Worked over 13 sts.
1st row (right side) K1, [yf, skpo] twice, k8.
2nd row and every alt row P13.
3rd row K2, [yf, skpo] twice, k7.
5th row K3, [yf, skpo] twice, k6.
7th row K4, [yf, skpo] twice, k2, mb, k2.
9th row K3, [k2 tog, yf] twice, k6.
11th row K2, [k2 tog, yf] twice, k7.
13th row K1, [k2 tog, yf] twice, k8.
15th row [K2 tog, yf] twice, k9.
16th row P13.
These 16 rows form patt.

PANEL C
Worked over 11(13) sts.
1st row (right side) K4(5), k2 tog, yf, k5(6).
2nd row and every alt row P11(13).
3rd row K3(4), k2 tog, yf, k1, yf, skpo, k3(4).
5th row K2(3), k2 tog, yf, k3, yf, skpo, k2(3).

7th row K1(2), k2 tog, yf, k5, yf, skpo, k1(2).
8th row P11(13).
These 8 rows form patt.

PANEL D
Worked over 13(15) sts.
1st row (right side) K2(3), yf, skpo, k5, k2 tog, yf, k2(3).
2nd row and 6 foll alt rows P13(15).
3rd row K3(4), yf, skpo, k3, k2 tog, yf, k3(4).
5th row K4(5), yf, skpo, k1, k2 tog, yf, k4(5).
7th row K5(6), yf, sl 1, k2 tog, psso, yf, k5(6).
9th row K4(5), k2 tog, yf, k1, yf, skpo, k4(5).
11th row K3(4), k2 tog, yf, k3, yf, skpo, k3(4).
13th row K2(3), k2 tog, yf, k5, yf, skpo, k2(3).
15th row K13(15).
16th to 20th rows P13(15).
21st row K13(15).
22nd row P13(15).
23rd row K6(7), p1, k6(7).
24th row P5(6), k1, p1, k1, p5(6).
25th row K4(5), p1, k3, p1, k4(5).
26th row P3(4), k1, [p2, k1] twice, p3(4).
27th row K2(3), p1, k2, p1, k1, p1, k2, p1, k2(3).
28th row P1(2), k1, p2, k1, p3, k1, p2, k1, p1(2).
29th row K3(4), p1, [k2, p1] twice, k3(4).
30th row P2(3), k1, p2, k1, p1, k1, p2, k1, p2(3).

31st and 32nd rows As 25th and 26th rows.

33rd row K5(6), p1, k1, p1, k5(6).

34th row P4(5), k1, p3, k1, p4(5).

35th and 36th rows As 23rd and 24th rows.

37th row K6(7), p1, k6(7).

38th row P13(15).

39th row K13(15).

40th to 44th rows P13(15).

45th and 46th rows As 21st and 22nd rows.

47th to 70th rows Work 1st to 24th rows.

71st row K4(5), p1, [k1, p1] twice, k4(5).

72nd row P3(4), k1, [p1, k1] 3 times, p3(4).

73rd row K2(3), p1, [k1, p1] 4 times, k2(3).

74th row P1(2), k1, [p1, k1] 5 times, p1(2).

75th row As 73rd row.

76th row As 72nd row.

77th row As 71st row.

78th row As 24th row.

79th to 86th rows As 37th to 44th rows. These 86 rows form patt.

PANEL E

Worked over 15 sts.

1st row (right side) K6, k2 tog, yf, k7.

2nd row and every alt row P15.

3rd row K5, k2 tog, yf, k1, yf, skpo, k5.

5th row K4, k2 tog, yf, k3, yf, skpo, k4.

7th row K3, k2 tog, yf, k2, mb, k2, yf, skpo, k3.

9th row K2, k2 tog, yf, k7, yf, skpo, k2.

11th row K1, k2 tog, yf, k2, mb, k3, mb, k2, yf, skpo, k1.

12th row P15.

These 12 rows form patt.

BACK

With 3mm (No 11/US 2) needles cast on 101(109) sts.

K 7 rows.

Change to 3¼mm (No 10/US 3) needles.

1st row (right side) K.

2nd row [P11(13), k3, p13, k3] 3 times, p11(13).

3rd row Work 1st row of panel A, [k3, work 1st row of panel B, k3, work 1st row of panel A] 3 times.

The last row sets position of panels and forms garter st between panels. Work a further 59(69) rows in patt. K 2 rows. Work in yoke patt as follows:

1st row K2, p1, [k7, p1] to last 2 sts, k2.

2nd row [P1, k1] twice, [p5, k1, p1, k1] to last st, p1.

3rd row P1, [k3, p1] to end.

4th row P5, [k1, p1, k1, p5] to end.

5th row K6, p1, [k7, p1] to last 6 sts, k6.

6th row As 4th row.

7th row As 3rd row.

8th row As 2nd row.

9th row As 1st row.

10th row K.

11th row [K1, p1] twice, k11(13), p1, k1, p1, k13(15), p1, k1, p2, k4, p2, k1, p1, k15, p1, k1, p2, k4, p2, k1, p1, k13(15), p1, k1, p1, k11(13), [p1, k1] twice.

12th row K1, p1, k1, p13(15), k1, p15(17), k1, p1, k1, p4, k1, p1, k1, p17, k1, p1, k1,

p4, k1, p1, k1, p15(17), k1, p13(15), k1, p1, k1.

13th row [K1, p1] twice, work 1st row of panel C, p1, k1, p1, work 1st row of panel D, p1, k1, p2, sl next 2 sts onto cable needle and leave at front of work, k2, then k2 from cable needle, p2, k1, p1, work 1st row of panel E, p1, k1, p2, sl next 2 sts onto cable needle and leave at back of work, k2, then k2 from cable needle, p2, k1, p1, work 1st row of panel D, p1, k1, p1, work 1st row of panel C, [p1, k1] twice.

14th row [K1, p1] twice, work 2nd row of panel C, p1, k1, p1, work 2nd row of panel D, [p1, k1] twice, p4, [k1, p1] twice, work 2nd row of panel E, [p1, k1] twice, p4, [k1, p1] twice, work 2nd row of panel D, p1, k1, p1, work 2nd row of panel C, [p1, k1] twice.

The last 2 rows set position of panels and last 4 rows form cable panel and moss st between panels. Patt a further 78(82) rows.

Shape Shoulders

Cast off 14(16) sts at beg of next 2 rows and 15(16) sts at beg of foll 2 rows. Leave rem 43(45) sts on a holder.

FRONT

Work as given for Back until Front is 14(16) rows less than Back to shoulder shaping, ending with a wrong side row.

Shape Neck

Next row Patt 40(43), turn.

Work on this set of sts only. Keeping patt correct, cast off 4 sts at beg of next row. Dec one st at neck edge on next 7 rows. 29(32) sts. Patt 5(7) rows.

Shape Shoulder

Cast off 14(16) sts at beg of next row. Work 1 row. Cast off rem 15(16) sts. With right side facing, slip centre 21(23) sts onto a holder, rejoin yarn to rem sts and patt to end. Complete to match first side.

SLEEVES

With 3mm (No 11/US 2) needles cast on 43(45) sts.

1st rib row (right side) K1, [p1, k1] to end.

2nd rib row P1, [k1, p1] to end.

Rep last 2 rows 7 times more, inc 6 sts evenly across last row. 49(51) sts.

Change to 3¼mm (No 10/US 3) needles.

Next row K3, work 1st row of panel B, k3, work 1st row of panel A, k3, work 1st row of panel B, k3.

This row sets position of panels and forms garter st between panels. Cont in patt, inc one st at each end of every foll 4th(5th) row until there are 77(83) sts, working inc sts into panel A patt, then into garter st. Cont straight until Sleeve measures 25(30)cm/10(12)in from beg, ending with a wrong side row. Cast off.

COLLAR

Join shoulder seams.

With set of four 3mm (No 11/US 2) double pointed needles and right side facing, sl first 10(11) sts at centre front neck onto a safety pin, join yarn and k rem 11(12) sts, k up 20(21) sts up right front neck, k back neck sts, k up 20(21) sts down left front neck, k 10(11) sts from safety pin. 104(110) sts. Work 6 rounds in k1, p1 rib, turn. K 23 rows.

Next row Cast off knitwise 2 sts, *sl st used in casting off back onto left needle, cast on 2 sts, cast off 4; rep from * until all sts are cast off.

TO MAKE UP

Sew on sleeves, placing centre of sleeves to shoulder seams. Join side and sleeve seams.

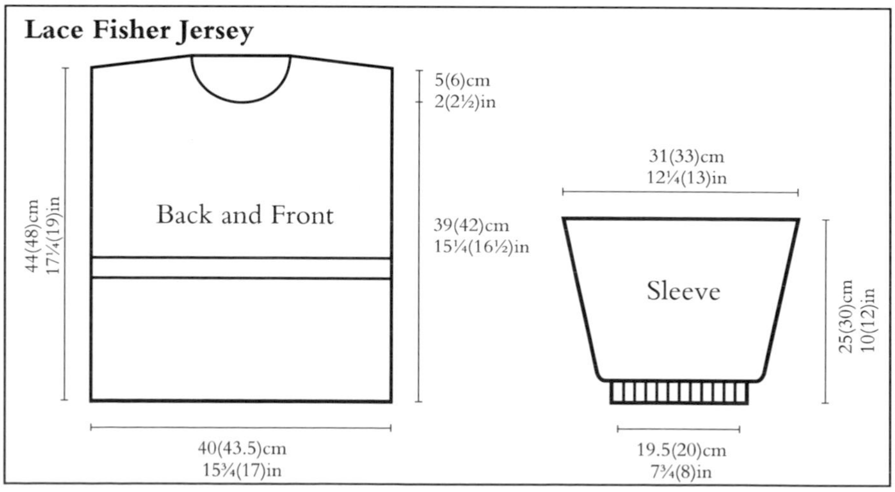

Lace Fisher Jersey

Back and Front

44(48)cm 17¼(19)in

40(43.5)cm 15¾(17)in

5(6)cm 2(2½)in

39(42)cm 15¼(16½)in

31(33)cm 12¼(13)in

Sleeve

25(30)cm 10(12)in

19.5(20)cm 7¾(8)in

Cabled Slipover page 26

MATERIALS

6(7:8) 50g balls of Rowan Cotton Glace in White (A).
1 ball of same in Black (B).
Pair each of 2¾mm (No 12/US 2) and 3¼mm (No 10/US 3) knitting needles.
Cable needle.

MEASUREMENTS

To fit age	2-3	4-5	6-7	years
Actual chest	72	80	88	cm
measurement	28½	31½	34½	in
Length	38	41	44	cm
	15	16	17¼	in

TENSION

28 sts and 36 rows to 10cm/4in square over pattern on 3¼mm (No 10/US 3) needles.

ABBREVIATIONS

C4F = sl next 2 sts onto cable needle and leave at front of work, k2, then k2 from cable needle.
Also see page 40.

BACK

With 2¾mm (No 12/US 2) needles and A, cast on 93(103:113) sts.
1st rib row (right side) P1, [k1, p1] to end.
2nd rib row K1, [p1, k1] to end.
Rep last 2 rows once more.
With B, k 1 row then rep 2nd rib row.
Cont in A only. K 1 row, then rep 2nd rib row.
Inc row Rib 6, [m1, rib 10] to last 7 sts, m1, rib 7. 102(113:124) sts.
Change to 3¼mm (No 10/US 3) needles.
1st row and 2 foll alt rows (wrong side) P4, [k1, p4, k1, p5] to last 10 sts, [k1, p4] twice.
2nd row K4, [p1, C4F, p1, k5] to last 10 sts, p1, C4F, p1, k4.
4th row K4, [p1, k4, p1, k5] to last 10 sts, [p1, k4] twice.
6th row P5, [k4, p7] to last 9 sts, k4, p5.
These 6 rows form patt. Cont in patt until Back measures 24(26:28)cm/9½(10¼:11)in from beg, ending with a wrong side row.
Shape Armholes
Keeping patt correct, cast off 10 sts at beg of next 2 rows. 82(93:104) sts. ★★ Cont straight until Back measures 37(40:43)cm/14¾(15¾:17)in from beg, ending with a wrong side row.
Shape Neck
Next row Patt 27(32:37), turn.
Work on this set of sts only. Dec one st at neck edge on next 4 rows. 23(28:33) sts.
Patt 1 row.
Shape Shoulder
Cast off 8(9:11) sts at beg of next row and foll alt row. Work 1 row. Cast off rem 7(10:11) sts.
With right side facing, slip centre 28(29:30) sts onto a holder, rejoin yarn to rem sts and patt to end. Complete to match first side.

FRONT

Work as given for Back to ★★.
Shape Neck
Next row Patt 40(46:51), turn.
Work on this set of sts only. Dec one st at neck edge on every foll alt row until 23(28:33) sts rem. Cont straight until Front matches Back to shoulder shaping, ending at armhole edge.
Shape Shoulder
Cast off 8(9:11) sts at beg of next row and foll alt row. Work 1 row. Cast off rem 7(10:11) sts.
With right side facing, sl centre 2(1:2) sts onto a safety pin, rejoin yarn to rem sts and patt to end. Complete to match first side.

NECKBAND

Join right shoulder seam.
With 2¾mm (No 12/US 2) needles, right side facing and A, k up 43(47:53) sts down left front neck, k0(1:0) st, [k2 tog] 1(0:1) time, mark last st, k up 42(47:52) sts up right front neck, 8 sts down right back neck, k centre back neck sts, k up 8 sts up left back neck. 130(140:152) sts.
1st rib row [P1, k1] to end.
2nd rib row Rib to 2 sts before marked st, skpo, k1, k2 tog, rib to end.
3rd row Rib to end.
4th row With B, k to 2 sts before marked st, skpo, k1, k2 tog, k to end.
5th row With B, as 1st row.
Cont in A, rep 4th row, then rib 3 rows, dec at centre front on right side row as before.
Cast off in rib, dec at centre front.

ARMBANDS

Join left shoulder and neckband seam
With 2¾mm (No 12/US 2) needles and A, k up 79(89:99) sts evenly around armhole edge including cast off sts at armholes. Work 3 rows in rib as given for Back welt. With B, k 1 row, then rib 1 row. Cont in A only, k 1 row, then rib 3 rows. Cast off in rib.

TO MAKE UP

Join side and armband seams.

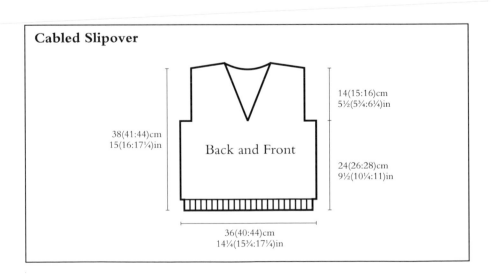

Cabled Slipover

Back and Front

38(41:44)cm
15(16:17¼)in

14(15:16)cm
5½(5¾:6¼)in

24(26:28)cm
9½(10¼:11)in

36(40:44)cm
14¼(15¾:17¼)in

Moss-stitch Tunic page 27

MATERIALS

8(10) 50g balls of Rowan DK
Handknit Cotton.
Pair each of 3¼mm (No 10/US 3)
and 4mm (No 8/US 6) knitting
needles.

MEASUREMENTS

To fit age	2-3	4-5	years
Actual chest	75	85	cm
measurement	29½	33½	in
Length	42	45	cm
	16½	17¾	in
Sleeve seam	22	26	cm
	8¾	10¼	in

TENSION

19 sts and 32 rows to 10cm/4in
square over moss st pattern on 4mm
(No 8/US 6) needles.

ABBREVIATIONS

See page 40.

BACK

With 4mm (No 8/US 6) needles cast on
71(81) sts.
1st row K1, [p1, k1] to end.
This row forms moss st patt. Cont in patt
until Back measures 42(45)cm/
16½(17¾)in from beg.
Shape Shoulders
Cast off 11(13) sts at beg of next 2 rows
and 12(14) sts at beg of foll 2 rows. Leave
rem 25(27) sts on a holder.

FRONT

Work as given for Back until Front
measures 37(39)cm/14½(15½)in
from beg.
Shape Neck
Next row Patt 30(34), turn.
Work on this set of sts only. Dec one st at
neck edge on every row until 23(27) sts
rem. Cont straight until Front matches
Back to shoulder shaping, ending at
side edge.
Shape Shoulder
Cast off 11(13) sts at beg of next row.
Work 1 row. Cast off rem 12(14) sts.
Slip 11(13) centre front sts onto a holder,
rejoin yarn at neck edge to rem sts and
patt to end. Complete as first side.

SLEEVES

With 4mm (No 8/US 6) needles cast on
31(35) sts.
Work in moss st patt as given for Back, inc
one st at each end of 9th row and every
foll 3rd(4th) row until there are 65(69) sts,
working inc sts into patt. Cont straight
until Sleeve measures 22(26)cm/8¾
(10¼)in from beg. Cast off.

COLLAR

Join right shoulder seam.
With 3¼mm (No 10/US 3) needles and
right side facing, k up 18(20) sts down left
front neck, moss st centre front sts, k up
18(20) sts up right front neck, moss st
centre back neck sts, inc one st in last st.
73(81) sts. Work 5cm/2in in moss st patt.

Change to 4mm (No 8/US 6) needles
and cont in patt for a further 6cm/
2¼in. Cast off loosely in patt.

TO MAKE UP

Join left shoulder and collar seam,
reversing seam on last 6cm/2¼in of
collar. Sew on sleeves, placing centre of
sleeves to shoulder seams. Beginning
3cm/1¼in up from lower edge, join side
seams, then sleeve seams.

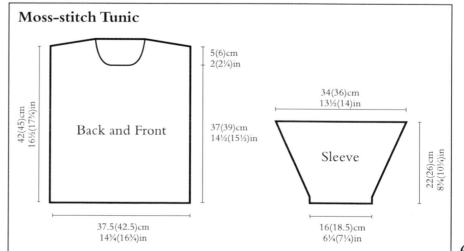

Moss-stitch Tunic

Back and Front

42(45)cm 16½(17¾)in

37.5(42.5)cm 14¾(16¾)in

5(6)cm 2(2¼)in

37(39)cm 14½(15½)in

Sleeve

34(36)cm 13½(14)in

16(18.5)cm 6¼(7¼)in

22(26)cm 8¾(10¼)in

Lace Panelled Jacket   page 27

MATERIALS

8(9) 50g balls of Rowan Cotton Glace.
Pair each of 2¾mm (No 12/US 2) and 3¼mm (No 10/US 3) knitting needles.
Cable needle.
12 buttons.

MEASUREMENTS

To fit age	2-3	3-4	years
Actual chest	66	77	cm
measurement	26	30½	in
Length	42	47	cm
	16½	18½	in
Sleeve seam	25	31	cm
	10	12¼	in

TENSION

25 sts and 34 rows to 10cm/4in square over st st on 3¼mm (No 10/US 3) needles.

ABBREVIATIONS

C4F = sl next 2 sts onto cable needle and leave at front of work, k2, then k2 from cable needle.
Also see page 40.

PANEL A

Worked over 11 sts.
1st row and every foll alt row (wrong side) P11.
2nd row K5, yf, skpo, k4.
4th row K3, k2 tog, yf, k1, yf, skpo, k3.
6th row K2, k2 tog, yf, k3, yf, skpo, k2.
8th row K1, k2 tog, yf, k5, yf, skpo, k1.
10th row K2 tog, yf, k7, yf, skpo.
These 10 rows form patt.

PANEL B

Worked over 7 sts.
1st row and every foll alt row (wrong side) P7.
2nd row K1, yf, skpo, k4.
4th row K2, yf, skpo, k3.
6th row K3, yf, skpo, k2.
8th row K4, yf, skpo, k1.
10th row K5, yf, skpo.
12th row K4, k2 tog, yf, k1.
14th row K3, k2 tog, yf, k2.
16th row K2, k2 tog, yf, k3.
18th row K1, k2 tog, yf, k4.
20th row K2 tog, yf, k5.
These 20 rows form patt.

BACK

With 2¾mm (No 12/US 2) needles cast on 85(99) sts.
1st row K1, [p1, k1] to end.
This row forms moss st. Moss st 9 rows more, inc one st at centre of last row. 86(100) sts.
Change to 3¼mm (No 10/US 3) needles.
1st row (wrong side) [Work 1st row of panel B] 0(1) time, *moss st 3, p4, moss st 3, work 1st row of panel A, moss st 3, p4, moss st 3*; work 11th row of panel B, moss st 3, p4, moss st 3, work 1st row of panel B, rep from * to *, [work 11th row of panel B] 0(1) time.
2nd row [Work 12th row of panel B] 0(1) time, *moss st 3, k4, moss st 3, work 2nd row of panel A, moss st 3, k4, moss st 3*; work 2nd row of panel B, moss st 3, k4, moss st 3, work 12th row of panel B, rep from * to *, [work 2nd row of panel

B] 0(1) time.
3rd row [Work 3rd row of panel B] 0(1) time, *moss st 3, p4, moss st 3, work 3rd row of panel A, moss st 3, p4, moss st 3*; work 13th row of panel B, moss st 3, p4, moss st 3, work 3rd row of panel B, rep from * to *, [work 13th row of panel B] 0(1) time.
4th row [Work 14th row of panel B] 0(1) time, *moss st 3, C4F, moss st 3, work 4th row of panel A, moss st 3, C4F, moss st 3*; work 4th row of panel B, moss st 3, C4F, moss st 3, work 14th row of panel B, rep from * to *, [work 4th row of panel B] 0(1) time.
These 4 rows set position of panels and form cable patt between panels. Patt a further 8 rows. Cast on 1 st at beg of next 2 rows. 88(102) sts. Working extra st at each end into moss st, cont in patt until work measures 41(46)cm/16(18)in from beg, ending with a wrong side row.
P 4 rows.

Shape Shoulders

Cont in garter st, cast off 14(16) sts at beg of next 2 rows and 13(16) sts at beg of foll 2 rows. Leave rem 34(38) sts on a holder.

LEFT FRONT

With 2¾mm (No 12/US 2) needles cast on 43(49) sts.
Work 9 rows in moss st as given for Back.
Next row Moss st 33(23), [m1, moss st 16] 0(1) time, m1, moss st 10. 44(51) sts.
Change to 3¼mm (No 10/US 3) needles.
1st row (wrong side) Moss st 6, work 1st row of panel B, moss st 3, p4, moss st 3, work 1st row of panel A, moss st 3, p4, moss st 3, [work 11th row of panel B] 0(1) time.
2nd row [Work 12th row of panel B] 0(1) time, moss st 3, k4, moss st 3, work 2nd row of panel A, moss st 3, k4, moss st 3, work 2nd row of panel B, moss st 6.
3rd row Moss st 6, work 3rd row of panel B, moss st 3, p4, moss st 3, work 3rd row of panel A, moss st 3, p4, moss st 3, [work 13th row of panel B] 0(1) time.

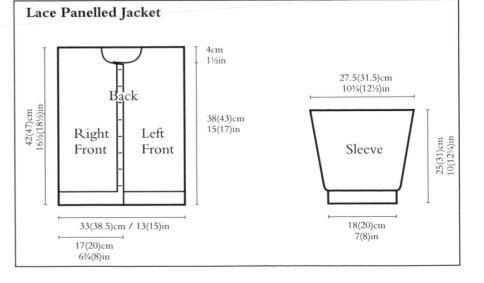

Lace Panelled Jacket

Back

4cm
1½in

38(43)cm
15(17)in

Right Front

Left Front

42(47)cm
16½(18½)in

33(38.5)cm / 13(15)in

17(20)cm
6¾(8)in

27.5(31.5)cm
10¾(12½)in

Sleeve

25(31)cm
10(12¼)in

18(20)cm
7(8)in

4th row [Work 14th row of panel B] 0(1) time, moss st 3, C4F, moss st 3, work 4th row of panel A, moss st 3, C4F, moss st 3, work 4th row of panel B, moss st 6.
These 4 rows set position of panels and form cable patt between panels. Patt a further 9 rows. Cast on 1 st at beg of next row. 45(52) sts. Working extra st into moss st, cont in patt until Front measures 38(43)cm/15(17)in from beg, ending with a wrong side row.
Shape Neck
Next row Patt to last 9 sts and turn; leave the 9 sts on a safety pin.
Keeping patt correct, cast off 3(4) sts at beg of next row and foll alt row. Dec one st at neck edge on next 3 rows. 27(32) sts.
Work straight for a few rows until Front measures 41(46)cm/16(18)in from beg, ending with a wrong side row. P 4 rows.
Shape Shoulder
Cast off 14(16) sts at beg of next row.
Work 1 row. Cast off rem 13(16) sts.
Mark front band to indicate position of 8 buttons; first one to came 3 rows up from lower edge, last one 1cm/¼ below top edge and rem 6 evenly spaced between.

RIGHT FRONT
With 2¾mm (No 12/US 2) needles cast on 43(49) sts.
Work 3 rows in moss st as given for Back.
Buttonhole row (right side) Moss st 2, k2 tog, yf, patt to end.
Moss st 5 rows.
Next row Moss st 10, m1, [moss st 18, m1] 0(1) time, moss st 33(21). 44(51) sts.
Change to 3¼ mm (No 10/US 3) needles.
1st row (wrong side) [Work 1st row of panel B] 0(1) time, moss st 3, p4, moss st 3, work 1st row of panel A, moss st 3, p4, moss st 3, work 11th row of panel B, moss st 6.
2nd row Moss st 6, work 12th row of panel B, moss st 3, k4, moss st 3, work 2nd row of panel A, moss st 3, k4, moss st 3, [work 2nd row of panel B] 0(1) time.
3rd row [Work 3rd row of panel B] 0(1) time, moss st 3, p4, moss st 3, work 3rd row of panel A, moss st 3, p4, moss st 3, work 13th row of panel B, moss st 6.
4th row Moss st 6, work 14th row of panel B, moss st 3, C4F, moss st 3, work 4th row of panel A, moss st 3, C4F, moss st 3, [work 4th row of panel B] 0(1) time.
These 4 rows set position of panels and form cable patt between panels. Complete as given for Left Front, making buttonholes to match markers and reversing all shapings.

SLEEVES
With 2¾mm (No 12/US 2) needles cast on 40(46) sts.
1st row [K1, p1] to end.
2nd row [P1, k1] to end.
These 2 rows form moss st. Moss st 5 rows more.
Next row Moss st 3(6), m1, moss st 7, work twice in next st, m1, moss st 10, m1, moss st 7, work twice in next st, m1, moss st 8, m1, moss st 3(6). 47(53) sts.
Change to 3¼mm (No 10/US 3) needles.
1st row P0(1), moss st 1(3), work 11th

row of panel B, moss st 3, p4, moss st 3, work 1st row of panel A, moss st 3, p4, moss st 3, work 1st row of panel B, moss st 1(3), p0(1).
2nd row K0(1), moss st 1(3), work 2nd row of panel B, moss st 3, k4, moss st 3, work 3rd row of panel A, moss st 3, k4, moss st 3, work 12th row of panel B, moss st 1(3), k0(1).
These 2 rows set position of panels and cable patt. Cont in patt, inc one st at each end of 3rd row and every foll 5th(6th) row until there are 73(83) sts, working inc sts into moss st on next 2 sts on **1st size** only, cable patt, then moss st. Cont straight until Sleeve measures 25(31)cm/10(12¼)in from beg, ending with a wrong side row.
Cast off.

COLLAR
Join shoulder seams.
With 2¾mm (No 12/US 2) needles and right side facing, slip 9 sts from right front safety pin onto needle, k up 18 sts up right front neck, k back neck sts, inc one st, k up 18 sts down left front neck, then k3, moss

st 6 sts from left front safety pin. 89(93) sts.
Next 2 rows Moss st to last 27(29) sts, turn.
Next 2 rows Moss st to last 24(26) sts, turn.
Next 2 rows Moss st to last 21(23) sts, turn.
Cont in this way, working 3 sts more at end of next 6 rows. Turn and moss st to end. Cast off 3 sts at beg of next 2 rows. Moss st 24 rows. Cast off in moss st.

TO MAKE UP
Sew on sleeves, placing centre of sleeves to shoulder seams. Beginning 22 rows up from lower edge, join side seams, then sleeve seams. Sew on buttons on left front edge and 2 buttons on each front side vent.

Black and White Cable Sweater

page 30

MATERIALS
9(10:11) 50g balls of Rowan Cotton Glace in Black (A).
3 balls of same in White (B).
Pair each of 3¾mm (No 9/US 4) and 2¾mm (No 12/US 2) knitting needles.
One 3¼mm (No 10/US 3) circular knitting needle.
Cable needle.

MEASUREMENTS

To fit age	4-5	6-7	8-9 years
Actual chest	81	88	96 cm
measurement	32	34½	38 in
Length	45	49	53 cm
	17¾	19¼	21 in
Sleeve seam	28	31	34 cm
(with cuff turn back)	11	12¼	13½ in

TENSION
33 sts and 35 rows to 10cm/4in square over cable pattern on 3¾mm (No 9/US 4) needles.

ABBREVIATIONS
See page 40.

BACK
With 2¾mm (No 12/US 2) needles and B, cast on 134(146:158) sts.
1st rib row P2, [k2, p2] to end.
2nd rib row K2, [p2, k2] to end.
Rib 2 rows more. Change to A and rib 2 rows. Change to B and rib 11 rows. Cont in A only.
Change to 3¾mm (No 9/US 4) needles.
1st row (right side) K2, [p2, k6, p2, k2] to end.
2nd row P2, [k2, p6, k2, p2] to end.
3rd and 4th rows As 1st and 2nd rows.
5th row K2, [p2, sl next 3 sts onto cable needle and leave at front of work, k3, then k3 from cable needle, p2, k2] to end.
6th row As 2nd row.
These 6 rows form cable patt. Cont in patt until Back measures 40(44:48)cm/15¾(17¼:19)in from beg, ending with a wrong side row.
Shape Neck
Next row Patt 51(55:59), turn.
Work on this set of sts only. Cast off 3 sts at beg of next row and 5 foll alt rows. 33(37:41) sts. Patt 4 rows straight. Cast off.
With right side facing, sl centre 32(36:40) sts onto a holder, rejoin yarn to rem sts and patt to end. Complete to match first side.

FRONT
Work as given for Back until Front measures 24(26:28)cm/9½(10¼:11)in from beg, ending with a wrong side row.
Shape Neck
Next row Patt 66(72:78), turn.
Work on this set of sts only. Dec one st at neck edge on every alt row until

63

33(37:41) sts rem. Work straight until Front measures same as Back to cast off edge, ending with a wrong side row. Cast off.

With right side facing, sl centre 2 sts onto a safety pin, rejoin yarn to rem sts, patt to end. Complete to match first side.

SLEEVES

With 2¾mm (No 12/US 2) needles and B, cast on 46(50: 54) sts.

Beg with 2nd(1st:2nd) rib row, work 4 rows in rib as given for Back welt. Change to A and rib 2 rows. Change to B and rib 27 rows. Cont in A only.

Change to 3¾mm (No 9/US 4) needles.

1st row (right side) P0(0:2), k0(2:2), [p2, k6, p2, k2] to last 10(12:14) sts, p2, k6, p2, k0(2:2), p0(0:2).

2nd row K0(0:2), p0(2:2), [k2, p6, k2, p2] to last 10(12:14) sts, k2, p6, k2, p0(2:2), k0(0:2).

These 2 rows set patt. Cont in patt as set, inc one st at each end of next row and

every foll alt row until there are 116(122:126) sts, working inc sts into patt. Cont straight until Sleeve measures 33(36:39)cm/13(14¼:15½)in from beg, ending with a wrong side row. Cast off.

NECKBAND

Join right shoulder seam. With 3¼mm (No 10/US 3) circular needle, right side facing and A, k up 71(75:79) sts down left front neck, k centre 2 sts (mark these 2 sts), k up 70(74:78) sts up right front neck, 18 sts down right back neck, k centre back neck sts dec 4 sts evenly, k up 19 sts up left back neck. 208(220:232) sts. Work backwards and forwards in rows. Change to B.

1st row [P2, k2] to 3 sts before marked sts, p1, sl next st onto cable needle and leave at front of work, sl next st onto right-hand needle, place st from cable needle and last st from right-hand needle back onto left-hand needle and p2 tog, p2, p2 tog, p1, [k2, p2] to end.

2nd row [K2, p2] to 2 sts before marked sts, k2 tog, k2, skpo, [p2, k2] to end. Work 15 more rows in rib as set, dec 2 sts at centre front as before.

Next row Rib to 2 sts before marked sts, dec 2 sts at centre, rib to last 66 sts, [k2, p2, k1, skpo, k2 tog, k1, p2, k2, p2] 4 times, k2.

Rib 3 rows.

Change to 2¾mm (No 12/US 2) needles.

Next row Rib to 2 sts before marked sts, dec 2 sts at centre, rib to last 58 sts, [k2, p2, skpo, k2 tog, p2, k2, p2] 4 times, k2. 148(160:172) sts.

Rib 3 rows, dec as before. Change to A and rib 2 rows, dec as before. Cont in B, rib 4 rows, dec as before. Cast off in rib dec as before.

TO MAKE UP

Join left shoulder and neckband seam. Sew on sleeves, placing centre of sleeves to shoulder seams. Join side and sleeve seams, reversing seams on cuffs. Turn back cuffs.

Entrelac Sweater   page 31

MATERIALS
13 50g balls of Rowan DK Handknit Cotton.
Pair each of 3¾mm (No 9/US 4) and 4mm (No 8/US 6) knitting needles.
Cable needle.

MEASUREMENTS

To fit age	5-6	years
Actual chest	92	cm
measurement	36	in
Length	50	cm
	19¾	in
Sleeve seam	33	cm
	13	in

TENSION

20 sts and 28 rows to 10cm/4in square over st st on 4mm (No 8/US 6) needles.

ABBREVIATIONS

C4B = sl next 2 sts onto cable needle and leave at back of work, k2, then k2 from cable needle;

C7B = sl next 4 sts onto cable needle and leave at back of work, k3, then [p1, k1] twice from cable needle;

C7F = sl next 3 sts onto cable needle and leave at front of work, [p1, k1] twice, then k3 from cable needle;

Cr7R = sl next 3 sts onto cable needle and leave at back of work, [p1, k1] twice, then k3 from cable needle;

Cr7L = sl next 4 sts onto cable needle and leave at front of work, k3, then [p1, k1] twice from cable needle.

Also see page 40.

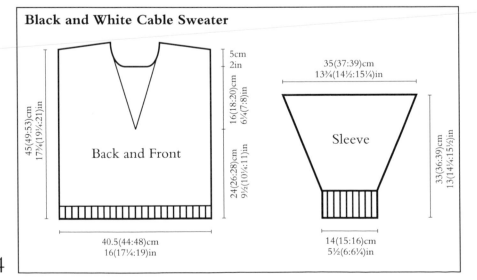

Black and White Cable Sweater

Back and Front

45(49:53)cm
17¾(19¼:21)in

40.5(44:48)cm
16(17¼:19)in

24(26:28)cm
9½(10¼:11)in

16(18:20)cm
6¼(7:8)in

5cm
2in

Sleeve

35(37:39)cm
13¾(14½:15¼)in

14(15:16)cm
5½(6:6¼)in

33(36:39)cm
13(14¼:15½)in

BACK

With 4mm (No 8/US 6) needles cast on 82 sts.

1st rib row (wrong side) P2, [k2, p4, k2, p2] to end.

2nd rib row K2, [p2, C4B, p2, k2] to end.

3rd rib row As 1st row.

4th rib row K2, [p2, k4, p2, k2] to end. Rib 7 rows more.

Next row K2 tog, * p2, [k2 tog] twice, p2, k2; rep from * to last 10 sts, p2, [k2 tog] twice, p2, k2 tog. 64 sts.

Work foundation triangles as follows:

First triangle

1st row P1, k1, turn.

2nd row K1, p1, turn.

3rd row P1, k1, p1, turn.

4th row P1, k1, p1, turn.

5th row [P1, k1] twice, turn.

Cont in this way, working 1 st more into moss st at end of every wrong side row until there are 16 sts on right-hand needle. Leave these sts on right-hand needle. Do not turn.

Second, third and fourth triangles

Work as given for first triangle. Turn.

**Left side edge triangle

1st row K2, turn.

2nd row P2.

3rd row Yon, k1, skpo, turn.

4th row and 5 foll alt rows P to last st, p tbl into yon of previous row.

5th row Yon, k2, skpo, turn.

7th row Yon, k3, skpo, turn.

9th row Yon, k4, skpo, turn.

11th row Yon, k5, skpo, turn.

13th row Yon, k6, skpo, turn.

15th row Yon, k7, sl 1, k2 tog, psso, turn.

16th row P to last st, p into front and back of yon of previous row.

17th row Yon, k9, skpo, turn.

18th row As 4th row.

Cont in this way, working one st more between inc at beg of row and dec at end of row until all sts of fourth foundation triangle have been worked off, ending with right side row. 16 sts. Leave these sts on right-hand needle. Do not turn.

First rectangle

With right-hand needle, k up 16 sts along other side of fourth foundation triangle, turn.

2nd row P8, k1, p7, turn.

3rd row K6, p1, k1, p1, k6, skpo, turn.

4th row P6, k1, [p1, k1] twice, p5, turn.

5th row K4, p1, [k1, p1] 3 times, k4, skpo, turn.

6th row P4, k1, [p1, k1] 4 times, p3, turn.

7th row K4, p1, [k1, p1] 3 times, k4, sl 1, k2 tog, psso, turn.

8th row As 4th row.

9th row As 3rd row.

Rep 2nd to 9th rows twice more, then work 2nd row again.

Next row K15, skpo. (All sts of third foundation triangle have been worked off.)

Leave these 16 sts on right-hand needle. Do not turn.

Second rectangle

With right-hand needle, k up 16 sts along other side of third foundation triangle, turn.

2nd row P16, turn.

3rd row K7, p1, k7, skpo, turn.

4th row P7, k1, p1, k1, p6, turn.

5th row K5, p1, k3, p1, k5, skpo, turn.

6th row P5, k1, [p2, k1] twice, p4, turn.

7th row K3, p1, k2, p1, k1, p1, k2, p1, k3, sl 1, k2 tog, psso, turn.

8th row P6, k1, p3, k1, p5, turn.

9th row K4, p1, [k2, p1] twice, k4, skpo, turn.

10th row P7, k1, p1, k1, p6, turn.

11th row K5, p1, k3, p1, k5, skpo, turn.

12th row P8, k1, p7, turn.

13th row K15, skpo, turn.

14th row P16, turn.

15th row K15, sl 1, k2 tog, psso, turn.

16th row P8, k1, p7, turn.

17th row K6, p1, k1, p1, k6, skpo, turn.

18th and 19th rows Work 8th and 9th rows.

20th row P4, k1, p2, k1, p1, k1, p2, k1, p3, turn.

21st and 22nd rows Work 5th and 6th rows.

23rd row K6, p1, k1, p1, k6, sl 1, k2 tog, psso, turn.

24th row As 8th row.

25th row As 3rd row.

26th row P16, turn.

27th row K15, skpo. (All sts of second foundation triangle have been worked off.)

Leave these 16 sts on right-hand needle. Do not turn.

Third rectangle

With right-hand needle, k up 16 sts along other side of second foundation triangle. Complete as given for first rectangle. (All sts of first foundation triangle have been worked off).

Right side edge triangle

With right-hand needle, k up 16 sts along other side of first foundation triangle.

2nd row P16, turn.

3rd row K14, skpo.

4th row P15, turn.

5th row K13, skpo.

6th row P14, turn.

7th row K12, skpo.

8th row P13, turn.

9th row K11, skpo.

10th row P12, turn.

11th row K9, sl 1, k2 tog, psso.

Cont in this way, dec one st at end of next 4 right side rows, ending with p row.

Next row K3, sl 1, k2 tog, psso.

Next row P4, turn.

Next row K2, skpo.

Next row P3, turn.

Next row K1, skpo.

Next row P2, turn.

Next row K2 tog, turn. *******

Fourth rectangle

With wrong side facing, sl first st from left-hand needle onto right-hand needle, then p up 17 sts more along inside edge of right side edge triangle, turn. 18 sts.

2nd row K6, p1, k4, p1, k6, turn.

3rd row P5, k1, p6, k1, p4, p2 tog, turn.

4th row K4, p1, k1, p1, C4B, p1, k1, p1, k4, turn.

5th row P3, k1, p1, k1, p6, k1, p1, k1, p2, p2 tog, turn.

6th row K2, p1, [k1, p1] twice, k4, [p1, k1] twice, p1, k2, turn.

7th row P3, k1, p1, k1, p6, k1, p1, k1, p2, p3 tog, turn.

8th row As 4th row.

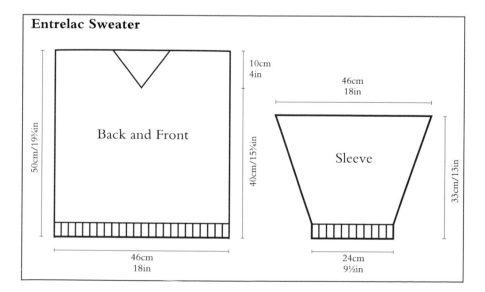

Entrelac Sweater

Back and Front

50cm/19¾in

46cm 18in

10cm 4in

46cm 18in

Sleeve

40cm/15¾in

33cm/13in

24cm 9½in

65

9th row As 3rd row.

Rep 2nd to 9th rows twice more, then work 2nd row again.

Next row P7, [p2 tog] twice, p6, p2 tog. (All sts of third rectangle have been worked off.)

Leave these 16 sts on right-hand needle. Do not turn.

Fifth rectangle

With right-hand needle, p up 18 sts along other side of third rectangle, turn.

2nd row P2, k3, [p1, k1] 4 times, k3, p2, turn.

3rd row K2, p3, [k1, p1] 4 times, p3, k1, skpo, turn.

4th and 5th rows Work 2nd and 3rd rows.

6th row As 2nd row.

7th row K2, p3, [k1, p1] 4 times, p3, k1, sl 1, k2 tog, psso, turn.

8th to 11th rows Rep 2nd and 3rd rows twice.

12th row P2, Cr7R, Cr7L, p2, turn.

13th row K2, [k1, p1] twice, p6, [k1, p1] twice, k1, skpo, turn.

14th row P2, [p1, k1] twice, k6, [p1, k1] twice, p2, turn.

15th row K2, [k1, p1] twice, p6, [k1, p1] twice, k1, sl 1, k2 tog, psso, turn.

16th row As 14th row.

17th to 20th rows Rep 13th and 14th rows twice.

21st row As 13th row.

22nd row P2, C7B, C7F, p2, turn.

23rd row As 7th row.

24th to 25th rows Rep 2nd and 3rd rows once.

26th row As 2nd row.

27th row K2, p2, p2 tog, [p1, k1] 3 times, p2 tog, p2, k1, skpo. (All sts of second rectangle have been worked off.)

Leave these 16 sts on right-hand needle. Do not turn.

Sixth rectangle

With right-hand needle, p up 18 sts along other side of second rectangle, turn. Complete as given for fourth rectangle. (All sts of first rectangle have been worked off).

Seventh rectangle

With right-hand needle, p up 18 sts along other side of first rectangle, turn. Complete as given for fifth rectangle. (All sts of left side edge triangle have been worked off). Turn.★★

Noting that sts will be picked up and worked off from seventh, sixth, fifth and fourth rectangles instead of triangles, rep from ★★ to ★★ twice more ★★★★, then from ★★ to ★★★.

Work top edge triangles as follows:

First top triangle

With wrong side facing, sl first st from left-hand needle onto right-hand needle, then p up 15 sts more along inside edge of side edge triangle, turn. 16 sts.

2nd row [P1, k1] 8 times, turn.

3rd row P2 tog, [k1, p1] 6 times, k1, p2 tog, turn.

4th row [P1, k1] 7 times, p1, turn.

5th row K2 tog, [p1, k1] 6 times, p2 tog, turn.

6th row [P1, k1] 6 times, p2 tog, turn.

7th row K2 tog, [p1, k1] 5 times, p3 tog, turn.

8th row Moss st 12, turn.

9th row P2 tog, moss st 9, p2 tog, turn.

10th row Moss st 11, turn.

11th row K2 tog, moss st 8, p2 tog, turn.

12th row Moss st 10, turn.

13th row P2 tog, moss st 7, p2 tog, turn.

14th row Moss st 7, k2 tog, turn.

Next 2 rows P2 tog, moss st 5, p3 tog, turn, moss st 7, turn.

Next 2 rows K2 tog, moss st 4, p2 tog, turn, moss st 6, turn.

Next 2 rows P2 tog, moss st 3, p2 tog, turn, moss st 5, turn.

Next 2 rows K2 tog, moss st 2, p2 tog, turn, moss st 4, turn.

Next 2 rows P2 tog, moss st 1, p3 tog, turn, moss st 3, turn.

Next 2 rows K2 tog, p2 tog, turn, moss 2, turn.

Next row Sl 1, p2 tog, psso.

Leave rem st on right-hand needle. Do not turn.

Second, third and fourth top triangles

With right-hand needle, p up 15 sts more along rectangle edge. 16 sts.

Complete as given for first top triangle. Fasten off.

FRONT

Work as given for Back to ★★★★, then work left side edge triangle and first rectangle. Turn.

Shape Neck

1st row K1, p1, turn.

2nd row P1, k1, turn.

3rd row K1, p2 tog, turn.

4th row Moss st 2, turn.

5th row Yon, moss st 1, p2 tog, turn.

6th row Moss st 2, p tbl into yon of previous row, turn.

7th row Moss st 2, p2 tog, turn.

8th row Moss st 3, turn.

9th row Yon, moss st 2, p3 tog, turn.

10th row Moss st 3, k tbl last st.

11th row Moss st 3, p2 tog, turn.

12th row Moss st 4, turn.

13th row Yon, moss st 3, p2 tog, turn.

14th row Moss st 4, p tbl last st, turn.

15th row Moss st, 4, p2 tog, turn.

16th row Moss st 5, turn.

17th to 20th rows Rep 15th and 16th rows twice.

21st row As 15th row.

22nd row Moss st 3, k2 tog, turn.

23rd row Moss st 3, p2 tog, turn.

24th row Moss st 2, p2 tog, turn.

25th row Moss st 2, p2 tog, turn.

26th row Moss st 1, k2 tog, turn.

27th row Sl 1, p2 tog, psso.

Do not turn. Work top edge triangle as given for fourth top edge triangle on Back. Fasten off.

With right side facing, sl 16 sts of next rectangle onto a holder, rejoin yarn to top and work third rectangle, right side edge triangle then first top edge triangle.

With right-hand needle, p up 15 sts more along edge of rectangle, turn.

2nd row K2 tog, [p1, k1] 7 times.

3rd row P2 tog, [k1, p1] 5 times, k1, p2 tog, turn.

4th row K2 tog moss st to end.

5th row K2 tog, moss st 8, p2 tog, turn.

Cont in this way, dec one st at beg of next row and at each end of foll row until 3 sts rem. Work 3 tog and fasten off.

PANEL A

Worked over 18 sts.

1st row (wrong side) P6, k1, p4, k1, p6.

2nd row K5, p1, k1, C4B, k1, p1, k5.

3rd row P4, [k1, p1, k1, p4] twice.

4th row K3, p1, k1, p1, k6, p1, k1, p1, k3.

5th row P2, [k1, p1] twice, k1, p4, k1, [p1, k1] twice, p2.

6th row K3, [p1, k1] twice, C4B, [k1, p1] twice, k3.

7th row As 3rd row.

8th row K5, p1, k6, p1, k5.

These 8 rows form patt.

PANEL B

Worked over 18 sts.

1st row (wrong side) K2, p3, [k1, p1] 4 times, p3, k2.

2nd row P2, k3, [p1, k1] 4 times, k3, p2.

3rd to 8th rows Rep 1st and 2nd row 3 times.

9th row As 1st row.

10th row P2, Cr7R, Cr7L, p2.

11th row K2, [k1, p1] twice, p6, [k1, p1] twice, k2.

12th row P2, [p1, k1] twice, k6, [p1, k1] twice, p2.

13th to 18th rows Rep 11th and 12th rows 3 times.

19th row As 11th row.

20th row P2, C7B, C7F, p2.

These 20 rows form patt.

PANEL C

Worked over 7 sts.

1st row (right side) P1, k6.

2nd row P5, k1, p1.

3rd row P1, k1, p1, k4.

4th row P3, [k1, p1] twice.

5th row P1, [k1, p1] twice, k2.

6th row As 4th row.

7th row As 3rd row.

8th row As 2nd row.

These 8 rows form patt.

PANEL D

Worked over 7 sts.

1st row (right side) K6, p1.

2nd row P1, k1, p5.

3rd row K4, p1, k1, p1.

4th row [P1, k1] twice, p3.

5th row K2, [p1, k1] twice, p1.

6th row As 4th row.

7th row As 3rd row.

8th row As 2nd row.

These 8 rows form patt.

SLEEVES

With 3¾mm (No 9/US 4) needles cast on 46 sts.

1st rib row (wrong side) K2, [p2, k2, p4, k2] to last 4 sts, p2, k2.

2nd rib row P2, [k2, p2, C4B, p2] to last 4 sts, k2, p2.

3rd rib row As 1st row.

4th rib row P2, [k2, p2, k4, p2] to last 4 sts, k2, p2.

Rib 11 rows more.

Next row Rib 6, m1, [rib 4, m1] twice, rib 8, m1, rib 2, m1, rib 8, [m1, rib 4] twice, m1, rib 6. 54 sts.

Change to 4mm (No 8/US 6) needles.

1st row Work 1st row of panel A, panel B and panel A.

This row sets position of panels. Cont in patt as set, inc one st at each end of 2nd row and every foll 3rd row until there are 98 sts, working inc sts into panel C at left side edge and panel D at right side edge, then into moss st. Cont straight until Sleeve measures 33cm/13in from beg, ending with a wrong side row. Cast off.

FRONT NECKBAND

With 3¾mm (No 9/US 4) needles and wrong side of front facing, sl the 16 sts on a holder onto needle, p up 2 sts at centre, then 16 sts along edge of following rectangle. 34 sts.

Next row P2, [k2, p2] 3 times, k1, k2 tog, skpo, k1, [p2, k2] 3 times, p2.

Next row K2, [p2, k2] 3 times, p2 tog tbl, p2 tog, [k2, p2] 3 times, k2.

Cast off in rib.

COLLAR

Join shoulder seams.

With 4mm (No 8/US 6) needles and wrong side facing , k up 25 sts up left front neck, 32 sts across centre back neck and 25 sts down right front neck. 82 sts.

Beg with a 2nd row, work 16 rows in rib as given for Back welt. Cast off in rib.

TO MAKE UP

Sew on sleeves, placing centre of sleeves to shoulder seams. Join side and sleeve seams. Sew row ends of front neckband to collar.

Striped Top with Beret and Sandals and Baby Blanket page 32

MATERIALS

Top 3(3:4) 50g balls of Rowan Cotton Glace in each of Navy (A) and Cream (B).
Pair of 3¼mm (No 10/US 3) double pointed knitting needles.
Pair each of 2¾mm (No 12/US 1) and 3mm (No 11/US 2) knitting needles.
8 buttons.

Beret 2 50g balls of Rowan Cotton Glace in Navy (A).
Oddment of same in Red.
Pair of 2¾mm (No 12/US 2) knitting needles.

Sandals 1 50g ball of Rowan Cotton Glace.
Pair of 2¾mm (No 12/US 2) knitting needles.
2 buttons.

Blanket 6 50g balls of Rowan Cotton Glace in Cream (A).
1 ball of same in each of Navy and Red.
Pair of 3¼mm (No 10/US 3) knitting needles.
Cable needle.

MEASUREMENTS

Top

To fit age	3-6	6-9	9-12months	
Actual chest	60	64	68	cm
measurement	23½	25	27	in
Length	28	30	33	cm
	11	11¾	12¾	in
Sleeve seam	17	19	21	cm
	6¾	7½	8¼	in

Beret and Sandals

To fit age	3-12	months

Blanket

Approximately
55cm x 70cm/21½in x 27¼in.

TENSION

25 sts and 34 rows to 10cm/4in square over st st on 3¼mm (No 10/US 3) needles.

ABBREVIATIONS

C4F = sl next 2 sts onto cable needle and leave at front of work, k2, then k2 from cable needle.
Also see page 40.

NOTES

Read charts from right to left on right side rows and from left to right on wrong side rows. When working pattern from charts, use separate lengths of contrast colours for each coloured area and twist yarns together on wrong side at joins to avoid holes.

STRIPED TOP

BACK AND FRONT (ALIKE)

With 2¾mm (No 12/US 1) needles and A, cast on 75(81:85) sts.

K 7 rows.

Change to 3¼mm (No 10/US 3) double pointed needles.

Next row (right side) K4, turn.

Work on these 4 sts only. K 5 rows. Leave these sts on a safety pin.

With right side facing, join B to rem sts, k to last 4 sts, turn.

Work on this set of 67(73:77) sts only in stripe patt as follows:

1st row Return to beg of last row, with A, k to end.

2nd row With B, p to end.

3rd row Return to beg of last row, with A, p to end.

4th row With B, k to end.

The last 4 rows form stripe patt. Patt a further 1 row. Leave these sts on a spare needle.

With right side facing, rejoin A to rem 4 sts and k 6 rows. Slip these sts onto needle holding centre sts.

With wrong side facing and B, p across all sts.

Beg with a 3rd row, cont in stripe patt until work measures approximately 19(21:23)cm/7½(8¼:9)in from beg, ending with 3rd row of stripe patt.

Next row With B, k6, p5, k to last 11 sts, p5, k6.

Next row Return to beg of last row, with A, k6, p5, k to last 11 sts, p5, k6.

Next row With B, p6, k5, p to last 11 sts, k5, p6.

Next row Return to beg of last row, with A, p6, k5, p to last 11 sts, k5, p6.

Rep last 4 rows for a further 5(5:6)cm/2(2:2¼)in, ending with 4th row of the last 4 rows. Cont in st st only and stripe patt, work as follows:

Shape Neck

Next row Patt 23(25:26), turn.

Work on this set of sts only for 7 rows. Cast off.

With right side facing, slip centre 29(31:33) sts onto a holder, rejoin yarn to rem sts, patt to end. Complete as first side.

SLEEVES

With 2¾mm (No 12/US 1) needles and A, cast on 38(40:42) sts.

K 7 rows, inc 4 sts evenly across last row. 42(44:46) sts.

Change to 3¼mm (No 10/US 3) needles.

Work in stripe patt as given for Back, inc

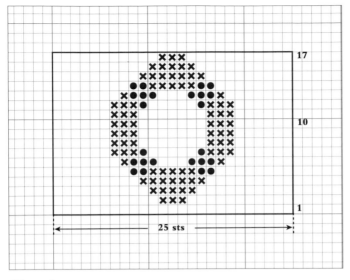

Chart 1

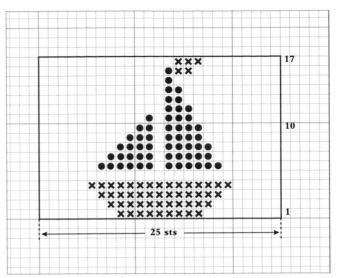

Chart 2

KEY

☐ Cream (A)
☒ Navy
● Red

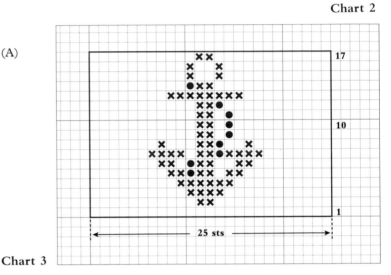

Chart 3

one st at each end of 3rd row and every foll 5th(4th:4th) row until there are 60(66:70) sts. Cont straight until Sleeve measures 17(19:21)cm/6¾ (7½:8¼)in from beg. Cast off.

BUTTONHOLE BANDS

With 3mm (No 11/US 2) needles, A and right side facing, k up 22(24:25) sts along left front shoulder. K 1 row.
Buttonhole row K4(6:7), [yf, k2 tog, k5] twice, yf, k2 tog, k2.
K 3 rows. Cast off.
Work right front shoulder band in same way, reversing buttonhole row as follows:
Buttonhole row K2, skpo, yf, [k5, skpo, yf] twice, k4(6:7).

BUTTON BANDS

With 3mm (No 11/US 2) needles, A and right side facing, k up 22(24: 25) sts along left back shoulder. K 5 rows. Cast off.
Work right back shoulder band in same way.

NECKBANDS

With 3mm (No 11/US 2) needles, A and right side facing, k up 10 sts down left front neck, k centre front neck sts, k up 10 sts up right front neck. 49(51:53) sts.
K 1 row.
Buttonhole row K2, yf, k2 tog, k4, skpo, k2 tog, k25(27:29), skpo, k2 tog, k4, skpo, yf, k2.
K 1 row.
Next row K7, skpo, k2 tog, k23(25:27), skpo, k2 tog, k7.
K 1 row. Cast off, dec at corners as before.
Work back neckband to match, omitting buttonholes.

TO MAKE UP

Lap buttonhole band over button band at shoulders and catch together at side edges. Sew on sleeves, placing centre of sleeves in line with buttonholes. Join side edgings to main parts. Beginning at top of side edgings, join side seams, then sleeve seams. Sew on buttons.

BERET

With 2¾mm (No 12/US 2) needles and A, cast on 76 sts.
K 5 rows.
Next row K5, [m1, k1, m1, k10] 6 times, m1, k1, m1, k4.
K 4 rows.
Next row K5, [m1, k1, m1, k12] 6 times, m1, k1, m1, k6.
K 4 rows.
Next row K7, [m1, k1, m1, k14] 6 times, m1, k1, m1, k6.
K 4 rows.
Next row K7, [m1, k1, m1, k16] 6 times,

m1, k1, m1, k8.
Cont in this way, inc 14 sts as set on 2 foll 5th rows. 160 sts. K 4 rows.
Next row K8, [k2 tog, k1, k2 tog, k18] 6 times, k2 tog, k1, k2 tog, k9.
K 4 rows.
Next row K8, [k2 tog, k1, k2 tog, k16] 6 times, k2 tog, k1, k2 tog, k7.
K 4 rows.
Next row K6, [k2 tog, k1, k2 tog, k14] 6 times, k2 tog, k1, k2 tog, k7.
K 4 rows.
Next row K6, [k2 tog, k1, k2 tog, k12] 6 times, k2 tog, k1, k2 tog, k5.
Cont in this way, dec 14 sts as set on every

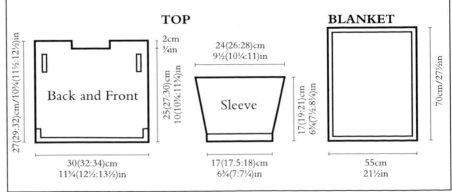

Striped Top with Beret and Sandals and Baby Blanket

TOP

Back and Front
27(29:32)cm/10¾(11½:12½)in
30(32:34)cm 11¾(12½:13½)in

Sleeve
2cm ¾in
24(26:28)cm 9½(10¼:11)in
25(27:30)cm 10(10¾:11¾)in
17(19:21)cm 6¾(7½:8¼)in
17(17.5:18)cm 6¾(7:7¼)in

BLANKET

70cm/27½in
55cm 21½in

68

5th row until 34 sts rem. K 1 row.
Next row [K2 tog] to end.
Next row K1, [k2 tog] to end.
Break off yarn, thread end through rem sts, pull up and secure. Join seam. With Red, make a small pom-pon and attach to top of beret.

SANDALS

RIGHT SANDAL
With 2¾mm (No 12/US 2) needles cast on 36 sts.
K 1 row.
1st row (right side) K1, yf, k16, yf, [k1, yf] twice, k16, yf, k1.
2nd row and 4 foll alt rows K to end, working k tbl into yf of previous row.
3rd row K2, yf, k16, yf, k2, yf, k3, yf, k16, yf, k2.
5th row K3, yf, k16, yf, [k4, yf] twice, k16, yf, k3.
7th row K4, yf, k16, yf, k5, yf, k6, yf, k16, yf, k4.
9th row K5, yf, k16, yf, [k7, yf] twice, k16, yf, k5.
11th row K22, yf, k8, yf, k9, yf, k22.
64 sts.
12th row As 2nd row.
K 12 rows.
Shape Instep
Next row K36, skpo, turn.
Next row Sl 1, p8, p2 tog, turn.
Next row Sl 1, k8, skpo, turn.
Rep last 2 rows 7 times more, then work first of the 2 rows again.
Next row Sl 1, k to end.
Next row K17, k2 tog, p8, skpo, k17.
44 sts.
Next row K24, turn.
Next row P4, turn.
Next row K4, turn.
Work in st st on these 4 sts only for 6cm/2¼in for front strap. Cast off.
With right side facing, rejoin yarn at base of strap, k up 12 sts along side edge of strap. Turn and cast off knitwise all sts at this side of strap.
With right side facing, rejoin yarn to top of other side of strap, k up 12 sts along side edge of strap, then k rem 20 sts. Cast off knitwise.
Join sole and back heel seam.
With 2¾mm (No 12/US 2) needles, right side facing and beginning and ending within 9 sts of back seam, k up 18 sts along heel for ankle strap. ★★
Next row Cast on 22, k to end, turn and cast on 4 sts.
Buttonhole row K to last 3 sts, k2 tog, yf, k1.
K 2 rows. Cast off.
Fold front strap over ankle strap to wrong side and slip stitch cast off edge in place.
Sew on button.

LEFT SANDAL
Work as given for Right Sandal to ★★.
Next row Cast on 4 sts, k to end, turn and cast on 22 sts.
Buttonhole row K1, yf, skpo, k to end.
Complete as Right Sandal.

BABY BLANKET

With 3¼mm (No 10/US 3) needles and A, cast on 150 sts.
1st row (right side) P1, k1, p1, C4F; ★ p1, [k1, p1] 15 times, C4F; rep from ★ 3 times more, p1, k1, p1.
2nd row P1, k1, p6, ★ k1, [p1, k1] 14 times, p6; rep from ★ 3 times more, k1, p1.
3rd row P1, k1, p1, k4, ★ p1, [k1, p1] 15 times, k4; rep from ★ 3 times more, p1, k1, p1.
4th row As 2nd row.
The last 4 rows form cable patt with moss stitch in between. Patt 2 rows.
7th row Patt 10, [k25, patt 10] 4 times.
8th row Patt 10, [p25, patt 10] 4 times.
9th to 14th rows Rep 7th and 8th rows 3 times.
15th row ★With A, patt 10, k 1st row of chart 1, with A, patt 10★, k 1st row of chart 2, with A, patt 10, k 1st row of chart 3, rep from ★ to ★.
16th row ★With A, patt 10, p 2nd row of chart 1, with A, patt 10 ★, p 2nd row of chart 3, with A, patt 10, p 2nd row of chart 2, rep from ★ to ★.
17th to 31st rows Rep last 2 rows 7 times more, then work 1st of the 2 rows again, but working 3rd to 17th rows of charts.
32nd row With A, work 8th row.
33rd to 41st rows With A, rep 7th and 8th rows 4 times, then work 7th row again.
42nd to 47th rows With A, work 2nd to 4th rows, then 1st to 3rd rows.
48th row With A, work 8th row.
49th to 55th rows With A, rep 7th and 8th rows 3 times, then work 7th row again.
56th row ★With A, patt 10, p 1st row of chart 2, with A, patt 10 ★, p 1st row of chart 1, with A, patt 10, p 1 st row of chart 3, rep from ★ to ★.
57th row ★With A, patt 10, k 2nd row of chart 2, with A, patt 10★, k 2nd row of chart 3, with A, patt 10, k 2nd row of chart 1, rep from ★ to ★.
58th to 72nd rows As 17th to 31st rows.
63rd to 82nd rows With A, rep 7th and 8th rows 5 times.
83rd to 88th rows With A, work 3rd and 4th rows, then 1st to 4th rows.

89th to 96th rows With A, rep 7th and 8th rows 4 times.
97th row ★With A, patt 10, k 1st row of chart 3, with A, patt 10 ★, k 1st row of chart 1, with A, patt 10, k 1st row of chart 2, rep from ★ to ★.
98th row ★With A, patt 10, p 2nd row of chart 3, with A, patt 10 ★, p 2nd row of chart 1, with A, patt 10, p 2nd row of chart 2, rep from ★ to ★.
99th to 123th rows As 17th to 41st rows.
124th row With A, work 4th row.
125th to 129th rows With A, work 1st to 4th rows, then 1st row.
130th row With A, work 8th row.
131st 137th rows With A, rep 7th and 8th rows 3 times, then work 7th row.
138th row ★With A, patt 10, p 1st row of chart 1, with A, patt 10★, p 1st row of chart 3, with A, patt 10, p 1st row of chart 2, rep from ★ to ★.
139th row ★With A, patt 10, k 2nd row of chart 1, with A, patt 10★, k 2nd row of chart 2, with A, patt 10, k 2nd row of chart 3, rep from ★ to ★.
140th to 164th rows As 58th to 82nd rows.
165th to 178th rows With A, work 1st to 14th rows.
179th row ★With A, patt 10, k 1st row of chart 2, with A, patt 10★, k st row of chart 3, with A, patt 10, k 1st row of chart 1, rep from ★ to ★.
180th row ★With A, patt 10, p 2nd row of chart 2, with A, patt 10★, p 2nd row of chart 1, with A, patt 10, p 2nd row of chart 3, rep from ★ to ★.
181st to 219th rows Work 17th to 55th rows.
220th row ★With A, patt 10, p 1st row of chart 3, with A, patt 10★, p 1st row of chart 2, with A, patt 10, p 1st row of chart 1, rep from ★ to ★.
221st row ★With A, patt 10, k 2nd row of chart 3, with A, patt 10★, k 2nd row of chart 1, with A, patt 10, k 2nd row of chart 2, rep from ★ to ★.
222nd to 252nd rows Work 58th to 88th rows.
With A, cast off, working 2 sts tog over each cable.

Denim Guernsey   page 32

MATERIALS

15 50g balls of Rowan Denim.
(see page 40).
Pair each of 3¼mm (No 10/US 3)
and 4mm (No 8/US 6) knitting
needles.
Cable needle.
2 buttons.

MEASUREMENTS

To fit age	6–8	years

The following measurements are after
the garment has been washed
according to the instructions given on
ball band.

Actual chest	102	cm
measurement	40	in
Length	52	cm
	20½	in
Sleeve seam	38	cm
	15	in

TENSION

20 sts and 28 rows to 10cm/4in square
over st st on 4mm (No 8/
US 6) needles before washing.

ABBREVIATIONS

C4F = sl next 2 sts onto cable needle
and leave at front of work, k2, then k2
from cable needle.
Also see page 40.

PANEL A
Worked over 13 sts.
1st row (right side) K1, p11, k1.
2nd row P1, k11, p1.
3rd row As 1st row.
4th row P13.
5th row K13.
6th row P6, k1, p6.
7th row K5, p1, k1, p1, k5.
8th row P4, k1, [p1, k1] twice, p4.
9th row K3, p1, [k1, p1] 3 times, k3.
10th row P2, k1, [p1, k1] 4 times, p2.
11th row K1, [p1, k1] 6 times.
12th row As 10th row.
13th row As 9th row.
14th row As 8th row.
15th row As 7th row.
16th row As 6th row.
17th row K13.
18th row P13.
These 18 rows form patt.

PANEL B
Worked over 11 sts.
1st row (right side) K1, p9, k1.
2nd row P1, k9, p1.
3rd row As 1st row.
4th row P7, k2, p2.
5th row K3, p2, k6.
6th row P5, k2, p4.
7th row K5, p2, k4.
8th row P3, k2, p6.
9th row K7, p2, k2.
10th row P1, k2, p8.
11th row K8, p2, k1.
12th row P2, k2, p7.
13th row K6, p2, k3.
14th row P4, k2, p5.
15th row K4, p2, k5.
16th row P6, k2, p3.
17th row K2, p2, k7.
18th row P8, k2, p1.
19th row K1, p2, k8.
Rows 4th to 19th form patt.

PANEL C
Worked over 15 sts.
1st row (right side) K1, p13, k1.
2nd row P1, k13, p1.

3rd row As 1st row.
4th row P15.
5th row K15.
6th row P7, k1, p7.
7th row K6, p1, k1, p1, k6.
8th row P5, k1, p3, k1, p5.
9th row K4, p1, [k2, p1] twice, k4.
10th row P3, k1, p2, k1, p1, k1, p2,
k1, p3.
11th row [K2, p1] twice, k3, [p1, k2]
twice.
12th row P4, [k1, p2] twice, k1, p4.
13th row K3, p1, k2, p1, k1, p1, k2,
p1, k3.
14th and 15th rows As 8th and 9th rows.
16th row P6, k1, p1, k1, p6.
17th row K5, p1, k3, p1, k5.
18th row As 6th row.
19th row K6, p3, k6.
20th row As 6th row.
21st row K15.
22nd row P15.
These 22 rows form patt.

BACK
With 3¼mm (No 10/US 3) needles cast
on 102 sts.
Beg with a k row, work 6 rows in st st.
1st rib row (right side) K2, [p2, k2]
to end.
2nd rib row P2, [k2, p2] to end.
Rep last 2 rows 4 times more.
Change to 4mm (No 8/US 6) needles.
Beg with a k row, work 17 rows in st st.
Next row P20, p twice in each of next
2 sts, p17, p twice in each of next 2 sts, p9,
p twice in next st, p10, p twice in each of
next 2 sts, p17, p twice in each of next
2 sts, p20. 111 sts.
1st row (right side) [P1, k1] twice, work
1st row of panel A, *k1, p1, k6, p1, k1*,
work 1st row of panel B, rep from * to *,
work 1st row of panel C, rep from * to *,
work 1st row of panel B, rep from * to *,
work 1st row of panel A, [k1, p1] twice.
2nd row [P1, k1] twice, work 2nd row of
panel A, *k1, p1, k1, p4, k1, p1, k1*, work
2nd row of panel B, rep from * to *, work
2nd row of panel C, rep from * to *, work

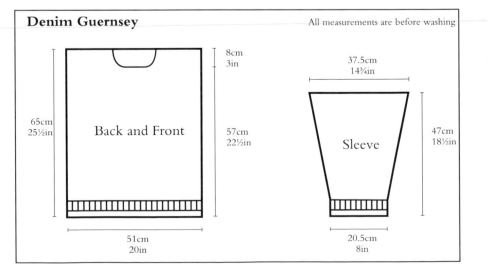

Denim Guernsey   All measurements are before washing

Back and Front — 65cm / 25½in, 8cm / 3in, 57cm / 22½in, 51cm / 20in

Sleeve — 37.5cm / 14¾in, 47cm / 18½in, 20.5cm / 8in

2nd row of panel B, rep from ★ to ★, work 2nd row of panel A, [k1, p1] twice.
3rd row [P1, k1] twice, work 3rd row of panel A, ★k1, p1, k1, C4F, k1, p1, k1★, work 3rd row of panel B, rep from ★ to ★, work 3rd row of panel C, rep from ★ to ★, work 3rd row of panel B, rep from ★ to ★ work 3rd row of panel A, [k1, p1] twice.
4th row [P1, k1] twice, work 4th row of panel A, ★k1, p1, k1, p4, k1, p1, k1★, work 4th row of panel B, rep from ★ to ★, work 4th row of panel C, rep from ★ to ★, work 4th row of panel B, rep from ★ to ★, work 4th row of panel A, [k1, p1] twice.
These 4 rows set position of panels and form cable and moss st patt between panels. Cont in patt as set until 132 rows of patt have been worked.
Work in ridge patt as follows:
1st row P.
2nd row K.
3rd and 4th rows P.
5th and 6th rows K.
7th row P.
8th and 9th rows K.
10th row P.
These 10 rows form ridge patt. Ridge patt 21 rows more. Leave these sts on a spare needle.

FRONT
Work as given for Back until 8 rows of ridge patt have been worked.
Shape Neck
Next row Patt 44, turn.
Work on this set of sts only. Dec one st at neck edge on 8 right side rows. 36 sts. Patt 6 rows. Leave these sts on a spare needle. With right side facing, sl centre 23 sts onto a holder, rejoin yarn to rem 44 sts, patt to end. Complete to match first side.

SLEEVES
With 3¼mm (No 10/US 3) needles cast on 38 sts.
Beg with a k row, work 6 rows in st st, then 10 rows in rib as given for Back, inc 3 sts across last row. 41 sts.
Change to 4mm (No 8/US 6) needles.
Beg with a k row, work in st st, inc one st at each end of 3rd row and 8 foll 4th rows. 59 sts. P 1 row.
1st row (right side) K1, work 1st row of panel B, ★k1, p1, k6, p1, k1★, work 1st row of panel C, rep from ★ to ★, work 1st row of panel B, k1.
2nd row K1, work 2nd row of panel B, ★k1, p1, k1, p4, k1, p1, k1★, work 2nd row of panel C, rep from ★ to ★, work 2nd row of panel B, k1.
3rd row K1, work 3rd row of panel B, ★k1, p1, k1, C4F, k1, p1, k1★, work 3rd row of panel C, rep from ★ to ★, work 3rd row of panel B, k1.
4th row K1, work 4th row of panel B, ★k1, p1, k1, p4, k1, p1, k1★, work 4th row of panel C, rep from ★ to ★, work 4th row of panel B, k1.
These 4 rows set position of panels and form cable and moss st patt between panels. Cont in patt, inc one st at each end of next row and every foll 6th row until there are 83 sts, working inc sts into cable and moss st patt. Patt 20 rows straight. Cast off.

NECKBAND
With right sides of back and front together (needles pointing in same direction) and taking one st from each needle and working them tog, cast off right shoulder sts.
With 3¼mm (No 10/US 3) needles and right side facing, k up 18 sts down left front neck, k centre front sts, k up 18 sts up right front neck, then k39 sts from centre of back, turn and cast on 4 sts for button band. 102 sts. K 1 row and p 2 rows.
1st rib row K6, [p2, k2] to last 4 sts, k4.
2nd rib row K4, p2, [k2, p2] to last 4 sts, k4.
Buttonhole row K1, k2 tog, yf, k1, rib to last 4 sts, k4.

Rib 5 rows, then rep the buttonhole row again. Rib 3 rows.
Next row K.
Next row K4, p94, k4.
Rep last 2 rows once more. Cast off.
With right sides of front and back together, cast off together left shoulder sts.

TO MAKE UP
Wash pieces according to the instructions given on ball band. When dry, sew on sleeves, placing centre of sleeves to shoulder seams. Join side and sleeve seams, reversing seams on first and last 6 rows. Sew on buttons.

Sweater with Nautical Motifs page 36

MATERIALS
6(7) 50g balls of Rowan DK Handknit Cotton in Black (A).
1 ball of same in each of Red (B), Blue (C) and White.
Pair each of 3¼mm (No 10/US 3) and 4mm (No 8/US 6) knitting needles.

MEASUREMENTS

To fit age	18–24	24–36	months
Actual chest	75	81	cm
measurement	29½	32	in
Length	38	41	cm
	15	16	in
Sleeve seam	22	24	cm
	8¾	9½	in

TENSION
20 sts and 28 rows to 10cm/4in square over st st on 4mm (No 8/US 6) needles.

ABBREVIATIONS
See page 40.

NOTES
Read charts from right to left on right side (k) rows and from left to right on wrong side (p) rows. When working in pattern from chart, use separate small balls of colours for each coloured area and twist yarns together on wrong side at joins to avoid holes.

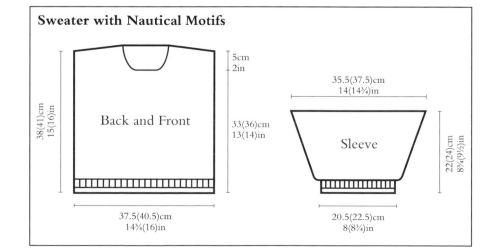

Sweater with Nautical Motifs

Back and Front
38(41)cm 15(16)in
37.5(40.5)cm 14¾(16)in
5cm 2in
33(36)cm 13(14)in

Sleeve
35.5(37.5)cm 14(14¾)in
20.5(22.5)cm 8(8¾)in
22(24)cm 8¾(9½)in

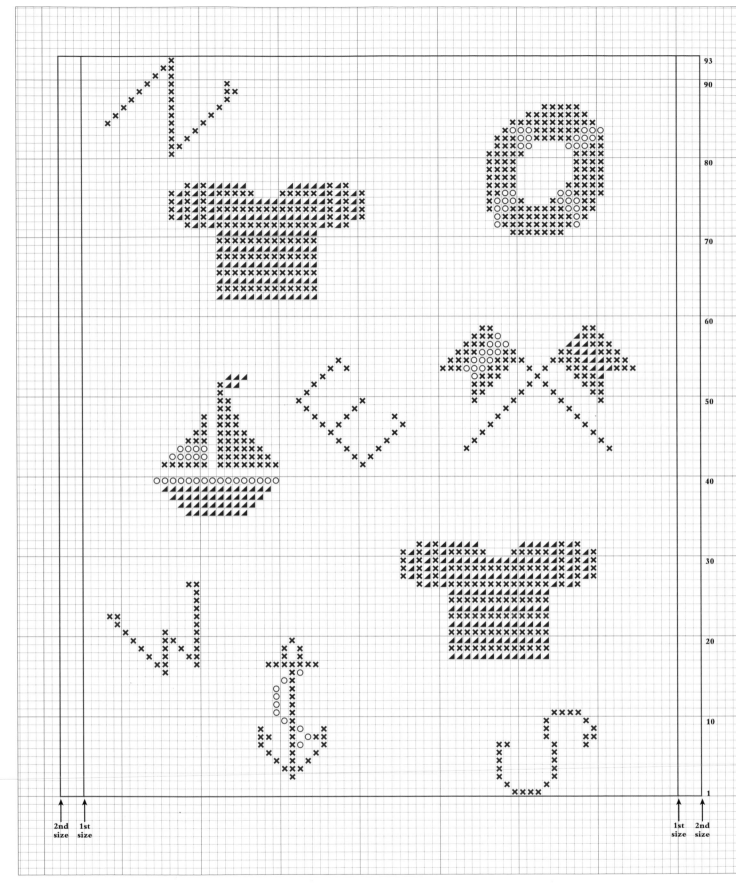

93
90
80
70
60
50
40
30
20
10
1

2nd
size
1st
size
1st
size
2nd
size

Chart 1

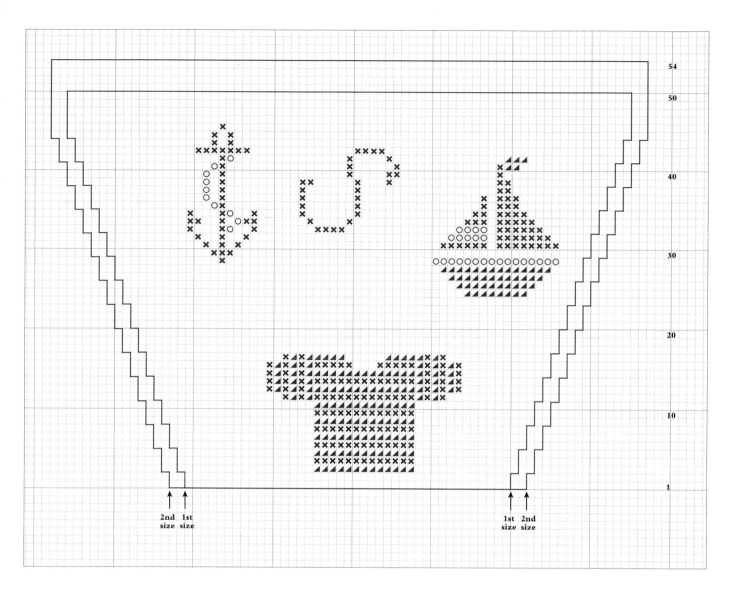

KEY

Chart 2

☐ Black (A)
◤ Red (B)
○ Blue (C)
✖ White

BACK

With 3¼mm (No 10/US 3) needles and B, cast on 74(78) sts.
Beg with a k row, work 4 rows in st st. Change to A.
1st rib row (right side) K2, [p2, k2] to end.
2nd rib row P2, [k2, p2] to end.
Rib 2 rows more, inc 1(3) sts evenly across last row. 75(81) sts.
Change to 4mm (No 8/US 6) needles. Beg with a k row, work 5(9) rows in st st. Work in st st and patt from chart 1 until 93rd row of chart has been worked. Cont in A only, work 2(6) rows.
Shape Shoulders
Cast off 12(13) sts at beg of next 4 rows.
Leave rem 27(29) sts on a holder.

FRONT

Work as given for Back until 81st(85th) row of chart has been worked.
Shape Neck
Next row Patt 30(32), turn.
Work in patt on this set of sts only. Dec one st at neck edge on next 6 rows. 24(26) sts. Patt 5(1) rows. Cont in A only, work 2(6) rows.
Shape Shoulder
Cast off 12(13) sts at beg of next row.
Work 1 row. Cast off rem 12(13) sts.
With right side facing, slip centre 15(17) sts onto a holder, rejoin yarn to rem sts and patt to end. Complete to match first side, reversing shoulder shaping.

SLEEVES

With 3¼mm (No 10/US 3) needles and C, cast on 34(38) sts.
Beg with a k row, work 4 rows in st st, then change to A and work 9(13) rows in rib as given for Back.
Next row Rib 2(3), inc in next st, [rib 4, inc in next st] 6 times, rib 1(4). 41(45) sts.
Change to 4mm (No 8/US 6) needles. Beg with a k row, work in st st and patt from chart 2, inc one st at each end of every 3rd row until there are 71(75) sts. Work 5(9) rows straight. Cast off.

NECKBAND

Join right shoulder seam.
With 3¼mm (No 10/US 3) needles, A and right side facing, k up 20 sts down left front neck, k front neck sts, k up 20 sts up right front neck, k back neck sts. 82(86) sts.
Beg with a 2nd row, work 7 rows in rib as given for Back. Change to B and beg with a k row, work 4 rows in st st. Cast off loosely.

TO MAKE UP

Join left shoulder and neckband seam, reversing seam on st st section of neckband. Sew on sleeves, placing centre of sleeves to shoulder seams. Join side and sleeve seams, reversing seam on first and last 4 rows.

73

MATERIALS

7(8) 50g balls of Rowan Cotton Glace in Red (A).
Small amount of same in Navy and Cream.
Pair each of 2¾mm (No 12/US 2) and 3¼mm (No 10/US 3) knitting needles.
Set of four in each of 3¼mm (No 10/US 3) and 3¾mm (No 9/US 4) double pointed knitting needles.
Cable needle.

MEASUREMENTS

To fit age	18–24	24–36 months	
Actual chest	63	70	cm
measurement	25	27½	in
Length	37	40	cm
	14½	15¾	in
Sleeve seam	20	24	cm
	8	9½	in

TENSION

25 sts and 34 rows to 10cm/4in square over st st on 3¼mm (No 10/US 3) needles.

ABBREVIATIONS

See page 40.

NOTES

Read charts from right to left on right side rows and from left to right on wrong side rows. When working colour motifs, use separate lengths of contrast colours for each coloured area and twist yarns together on wrong side at joins to avoid holes.

CABLE PANEL

Worked over 4 sts.
1st row (right side) K4.
2nd row P4.
3rd and 4th rows As 1st and 2nd rows.
5th row Sl next 2 sts onto cable needle and leave at front of work, k2, then k2 from cable needle.
6th row P4.
These 6 rows form patt.

TREE AND ANCHOR PANEL

Worked over 12 sts.
1st row (right side) K12.
2nd row P12.
3rd row K5, p2, k5.
4th row P4, k1, p2, k1, p4.
5th row K3, p1, k4, p1, k3.
6th row P2, k1, p2, k2, p2, k1, p2.
7th row K1, p1, [k2, p1] 3 times, k1.
8th row P3, k1, p4, k1, p3.
9th row K2, p1, k2, p2, k2, p1, k2.
10th row P1, k1, [p2, k1] 3 times, p1.
11th and 12th rows As 5th and 6th rows.
13th row K4, p1, k2, p1, k4.
14th row As 8th row.
15th row K12.
16th to 20th rows P12.
21st and 22nd rows As 1st and 2nd rows.
23rd row K12 sts of 1st row of chart 1.
24th row P12 sts of 2nd row of chart 1.
25th to 34th rows Rep 23rd and 24th rows 5 times, but working 3rd to 12th rows of chart 1.
35th row K12.
36th to 40th rows P12.
41st to 80th rows Work 1st to 40th rows, but using Cream instead of Navy and Navy instead of Cream on anchor motif. These 80 rows form patt.

BOAT AND DIAMOND PANEL

Worked over 13 sts.
1st row (right side) K13.
2nd row P13.
3rd row K13 sts of 1st row of chart 2.
4th row P13 sts of 2nd row of chart 2.
5th to 14th rows Rep 3rd and 4th rows 5 times, but working 3rd to 12th rows of chart 2.

15th row K13.
16th to 20th rows P13.
21st and 22nd rows As 1st and 2nd rows.
23rd row K6, p1, k6.
24th row P5, k1, p1, k1, p5.
25th row K4, p1, [k1, p1] twice, k4.
26th row P3, k1, [p1, k1] 3 times, p3.
27th row K2, p1, [k1, p1] 4 times, k2.
28th row P1, [k1, p1] 6 times.
29th row As 27th row.
30th row As 26th row.
31st row As 25th row.
32nd row As 24th row.
33rd row K6, p1, k6.
34th row P13.
35th row K13.
36th to 40th rows P13.
41st to 80th rows Work 1st to 40th rows but using Cream instead of Navy and Navy instead of Cream on boat motif. These 80 rows form patt.

BACK

With 3¼mm (No 10/US 3) needles and A, cast on 116(124) sts.
1st row (right side) [K1, p1] to end.
2nd row [P1, k1] to end.
These 2 rows form moss st. Moss st 4 rows more.
Beg with a k row, work in st st until work measures 6(9)cm/2¼(3½)in from beg, ending with a p row.
Inc row K11(15), [k2 tog] 12 times, k10, [k2 tog] 13 times, k10, [k2 tog] 12 times, k11(15). 79(87) sts.
P 1 row.
Next row [K1, p1] 0(2) times, k1, *p1, k1, p1, work 1st row of cable panel, p1, k1, p1, work 1st row of tree and anchor panel, p1, k1, p1, work 1st row of cable panel, p1, k1, p1*, work 1st row of boat and diamond panel, rep from * to *, k1, [p1, k1] 0(2) times.
This row sets position of panels and forms moss st between panels. Work a further 113 rows in patt.

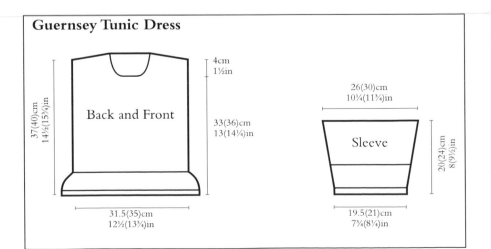

Guernsey Tunic Dress

Back and Front
37(40)cm
14½(15¾)in
4cm
1½in
33(36)cm
13(14¼)in
31.5(35)cm
12½(13¾)in

Sleeve
26(30)cm
10¼(11¾)in
20(24)cm
8(9½)in
19.5(21)cm
7¾(8¼)in

Chart 1

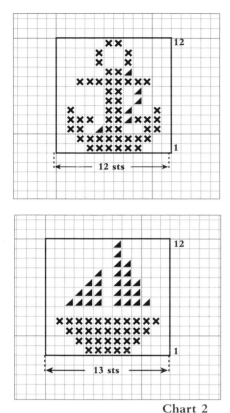

12 sts

Chart 2

13 sts

KEY

☐	Red (A)
☒	Navy
◣	Cream

Shape Shoulders
Cast off 12(14) sts at beg of next 2 rows and 12(13) sts at beg of foll 2 rows. Leave rem 31(33) sts on a holder.

FRONT
Work as given for Back until 100 rows of patt have been worked.
Shape Neck
Next row Patt 33(36), turn.
Work on this set of sts only. Keeping patt correct, dec one st at neck edge on next 9 rows. 24(27) sts. Patt 4 rows.
Shape Shoulder
Cast off 12(14) sts at beg of next row. Work 1 row. Cast off rem 12(13) sts. With right side facing, slip centre 13(15) sts onto a holder, rejoin yarn to rem sts and patt to end. Complete to match first side.

SLEEVES
With 2¾mm (No 12/US 2) needles and A, cast on 40(44) sts. Work 6 rows in moss st as given for Back welt.
Change to 3¼mm (No 10/US 3) needles.
Inc row K0(2) [k4, m1] 9 times, k4(6). 49(53) sts.
Beg with a p row, work 12 rows in st st, inc one st at each end of 2 foll 6th rows. 53(57) sts.
Inc row P6(8), [m1, p10] 4 times, m1, p7(9). 58(62) sts.
Next row P1, [k1, p1] 2(3) times, work 3rd row of cable panel, *p1, [k1, p1] 3 times, work 3rd row of cable panel; rep from * 3 times more, p1, [k1, p1] 2(3) times.

This row sets position of panels and form moss st between panels. Cont in patt, inc one st at each end of 6th(4th) row and every foll 8th(6th) row until there are 66(76) sts, working inc sts into moss st. Cont straight until Sleeve measures 20(24)cm/8(9½)in from beg, ending with a wrong side row. Cast off.

COLLAR
Join shoulder seams.
With set of four 3¼mm (No 10/US 3) double pointed needles and right side facing, sl first 6(7) sts at centre front neck onto a safety pin, join A yarn and k rem 7(8) sts, k up 17 sts up right front neck, k back neck sts, k up 17 sts down left front neck, k6(7) sts from safety pin. 78(82) sts.

Work 4 rounds in k1, p1 rib, inc one st at end of last round, turn.
Next row P1, k1, p1, k to last 3 sts, p1, k1, p1.
Next row P1, k1, p to last 2 sts, k1, p1.
Rep last 2 rows twice more.
Change to set of four 3¾mm (No 9/US 4) double pointed needles.
Rep last 2 rows 5 times more. Work 4 rows in moss st across all sts. Cast off loosely in moss st.

TO MAKE UP
Sew on sleeves, placing centre of sleeves to shoulder seams. Join side and sleeve seams.

Cable Sweater with Boats page 38

MATERIALS
10(11:12) 50g balls of Rowan Cotton Glace in Cream (A).
1 ball of same in each of Navy (B), Red (C) and Green (D).
Pair each of 3¾mm (No 9/US 4) and 2¾mm (No 12/US 2) knitting needles.
One 2¾mm (No 12/US 2) circular knitting needle.
Cable needle.

MEASUREMENTS

To fit age	4-5	6-7	8-9	years
Actual chest	79	86	93	cm
measurement	31	34	36½	in
Length	43	47	51	cm
	17	18½	20	in
Sleeve seam	26	29	32	cm
	10¼	11½	12½	in

TENSION
33 sts and 35 rows to 10cm/4in square over cable pattern on 3¾mm (No 9/US 4) needles.

ABBREVIATIONS
See page 40.

NOTE
When working in colour pattern, use separate lengths of contrast colours for each coloured area and twist yarns together on wrong side at joins to avoid holes.

Cable Sweater with Boats

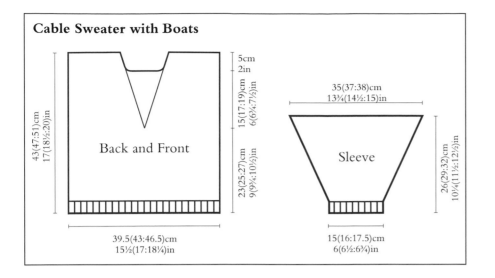

Back and Front

43(47:51)cm
17(18½:20)in

39.5(43:46.5)cm
15½(17:18¼)in

5cm
2in

15(17:19)cm
6(6¾:7½)in

23(25:27)cm
9(9¾:10½)in

Sleeve

35(37:38)cm
13¾(14½:15)in

26(29:32)cm
10¼(11½:12½)in

15(16:17.5)cm
6(6½:6¾)in

BACK
With 2¾mm (No 12/US 2) needles and B, cast on 130(142:154) sts.
1st rib row P2, [k2, p2] to end.
Change to A.
2nd rib row K2, [p2, k2] to end.
Rib 5 rows more. Change to C and rib 2 rows. Cont in A only, rib 6 rows.
Change to 3¾mm (No 9/US 4) needles.
1st row (right side) K2, p2, k2, [p2, k6, p2, k2] to last 4 sts, p2, k2.
2nd row P2, k2, p2, [k2, p6, k2, p2] to last 4 sts, k2, p2.
3rd and 4th rows As 1st and 2nd rows.
5th row K2, p2, k2, [p2, sl next 3 sts onto cable needle and leave at front of work, k3, then k3 from cable needle, p2, k2] to last 4 sts, p2, k2.

KEY

- ☒ Cream (A)
- ☐ Navy (B)
- ◪ Red (C)
- ⦿ Green (D)

6th row As 2nd row.
These 6 rows form cable patt. Cont in patt until Back measures 38(42:46)cm/15(16½: 18)in from beg, ending with a wrong side row.
Shape Neck
Next row Patt 49(53:57), turn.
Work on this set of sts only. Cast off 3 sts at beg of next row and 5 foll alt rows. 31(35:39) sts. Patt 4 rows straight. Cast off.
With right side facing, sl centre 32(36:40) sts onto a holder, rejoin yarn to rem sts and patt to end. Complete to match first side.

FRONT
Work as given for Back until Front measures 23(25:27)cm/9(10:10½)in from beg, ending with a wrong side row.
Shape Neck
Next row Patt 64(70:76), turn.
Work on this set of sts only. Dec one st at neck edge on next 4(2:0) rows, then on every alt row until 31(35:39) sts rem. Work straight until Front measures same as Back to cast off edge, ending with a wrong side

row. Cast off.
With right side facing, sl centre 2 sts onto a safety pin, rejoin yarn to rem sts, patt to end. Complete to match first side.

SLEEVES
With 2¾mm (No 12/US 2) needles and B, cast on 50(54:58) sts.
Beg with 1st(2nd:1st) rib row, work 1 row in rib as given for Back welt. Change to A and rib 6 rows. Change to D and rib 2 rows. Cont in A only, rib 6 rows.
Change to 3¾mm (No 9/US 4) needles.
1st row (right side) K0(0:2), p0(2:2), k2, [p2, k6, p2, k2] to last 0(2:4) sts, p0(2:2), k0(0:2).
2nd row P0(0:2), k0(2:2), p2, [k2, p6, k2, p2] to last 0(2:4) sts, k0(2:2), p0(0:2).
These 2 rows set patt. Cont in patt as set, inc one st at each end of next row and every foll alt row until there are 116(122:126) sts, working inc sts into patt. Cont straight until Sleeve measures 26(29:32)cm/10¼(11½:12½)in from beg, ending with a wrong side row.
Cast off.

NECKBAND
Join right shoulder seam. With 2¾mm (No 12/US 2) circular needle, right side facing and A, k up 70(76:82) sts down left front neck, k centre 2 sts (mark these 2 sts), k up 70(75:81) sts up right front neck, 18(19:19) sts down right back neck, k centre back neck sts dec 3(3:2) sts evenly, k up 18(19:19) sts up left back neck. 207(224:241) sts. Change to B. Work backwards and forwards in rows.
1st row P to 1 st before marked sts, sl next st onto cable needle and leave at front of work, sl next st onto right-hand needle, place st from cable needle and last st from right-hand needle back onto left-hand needle, [p2 tog] twice, p to end.
2nd row K to 1 st before marked sts, k2 tog, skpo, k to end.
3rd row Reading chart from right to left,

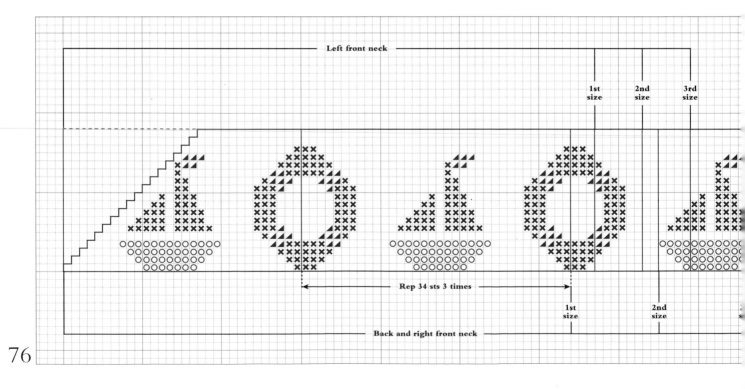

Left front neck

1st size   2nd size   3rd size

Rep 34 sts 3 times

1st size   2nd size

Back and right front neck

p 1st row of chart as indicated for back and right front neck to 1 st before marked sts, with B dec 2 sts at centre front as before, reading chart from left to right p 1st row of chart as indicated for left front neck.

4th row Reading chart from right to left, k 2nd row of chart as indicated for left front neck to 1 st before marked sts, with B dec 2 sts at centre front as before, reading chart from left to right, k 2nd row of chart as indicated for back and right front neck.

Work as set, dec 2 sts at centre front as before until 18th row of chart has been worked. Change to A, p 1 row, dec as before.

Next row *K1, k2 tog, p2, k2, [p2 tog, p1, k2] 0(1:1) time, p2*, rep from * to * 4(2:3) times more, k2(1:1), [k2 tog] 0(1:1) time, [p2, k2] 0(2:0) times, p1, dec 2 sts, p1, [k2, p2] 0(1:0) time, [k2 tog] 0(1:1) time, k2(1:1), **p2, [k2, p1, p2 tog] 0(1:1) time, k2, p2, k1, k2 tog**; rep from ** to ** 4(2:3) times more, [p1, p2 tog, k1, k2 tog] 10(12:12) times, p1(2: 1), [p2 tog] 1(0:1) time, k2(0:0). 134(144:156) sts. With A, work 3 more rows in rib as set, dec at centre front as before. Change to C and rib 2 rows, dec as before. Change to A and rib 4 rows, dec as before. Change to B and rib 1 row, dec as before. With B, cast off in rib, dec as before.

TO MAKE UP

Join left shoulder and neckband seam. Sew on sleeves, placing centre of sleeves to shoulder seams. Join side and sleeve seams.

Anchor Sweater
page 39

MATERIALS

7(8:10) 50g balls of Rowan DK Handknit Cotton in Cream (A).
1 ball of same in Black.
Pair each of 3¼mm (No 10/US 3), 3¾mm (No 9/US 4) and 4mm (No 8/US 6) knitting needles.
Cable needle.

MEASUREMENTS

To fit age	1-2	2-3	4-5	years
Actual chest	71	81	91	cm
measurement	28	32	36	in
Length	37	42	49	cm
	14½	16½	19¼	in
Sleeve seam	20	24	28	cm
	8	9½	11	in

TENSION

20 sts and 28 rows to 10cm/4in square over st st on 4mm (No 8/US 6) needles.

ABBREVIATIONS

C4F = sl next 2 sts onto cable needle and leave at front of work, k2, then k2 from cable needle.
Also see page 40.

NOTES

Read chart from right to left on right side (k) rows and from left to right on wrong side (p) rows. When working anchor motif, use small separate balls of colours for each coloured area and twist yarns together on wrong side at joins to avoid holes.

FRONT

With 3¾mm (No 9/US 4) needles and A, cast on 82(90:98) sts.
1st rib row (right side) K2, [p1, k4, p1, k2] to end.
2nd rib row P2, [k1, p4, k1, p2] to end.
3rd rib row K2, [p1, C4F, p1, k2] to end.
4th row As 2nd row.
Rep last 4 rows 2(3:3) times more.
Change to 4mm (No 8/US 6) needles.
Next row K0(16:0), k2 tog, [k6(6:14), k2 tog] to last 0(8:0) sts, k0(8:0). 71(81:91) sts.
Beg with a p row, work 5(9:13) rows in st st.
Next row K15(20:25)A, k 1st row of chart, with A, k to end.
Next row P15(20:25)A, p 2nd row of chart, with A, p to end.
Work a further 50(58:62) rows as set.
3rd size only
Cont in A only, work 10 rows.
All sizes
Continuing working from chart on 1st and 2nd sizes only until 64th row of chart has been worked, then cont in A only, work as follows:
Next row K6, p2, k4, p2, k to last 14 sts, p2, k4, p2, k6.
Next row P6, k2, p4, k2, p to last 14 sts, k2, p4, k2, p6.
Next row K6, p2, C4F, p2, k to last 14 sts, p2, C4F, p2, k6.
Next row P6, k2, p4, k2, p to last 14 sts, k2, p4, k2, p6.
Rep last 4 rows 4 times more.
Beg with a k row, cont in st st across all sts, work 4 rows.
Shape Neck
Next row K27(30:34), turn.
Work on this set of sts only. Dec one st at neck edge on every row until 17(20:24) sts rem. Work 1 row.
Shape Shoulder
Cast off 8(10:12) sts at beg of next row. Work 1 row. Cast off rem 9(10:12) sts. With right side facing, slip centre 17(21:23) sts onto a holder, rejoin yarn to rem sts, k to end.
Complete to match first side.

BACK

Work as given for Front to shoulder shaping omitting anchor motif and neck shaping, ending with a p row.
Shape Shoulders
Cast off 8(10:12) sts at beg of next 2 rows and 9(10:12) sts at beg of foll 2 rows.
Leave rem 37(41:43) sts on a holder.

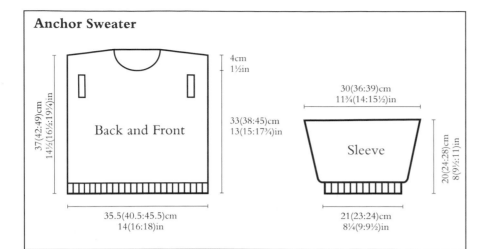

Anchor Sweater

Back and Front

37(42:49)cm
14½(16½:19¼)in

4cm
1½in

33(38:45)cm
13(15:17¾)in

35.5(40.5:45.5)cm
14(16:18)in

30(36:39)cm
11¾(14:15½)in

Sleeve

20(24:28)cm
8(9½:11)in

21(23:24)cm
8¼(9:9½)in

SLEEVES

With 3¼mm (No 10/US 3) needles and
A, cast on 34(34:42) sts.
Work 12(16:16) rows in rib as given for
Back welt, inc 8(12:6) sts evenly across last
row. 42(46:48) sts.
Change to 4mm (No 8/US 6) needles.
Beg with a k row, work in st st, inc one st
at each end of 3rd row and every foll
4th(3rd:3rd) row until there are 60(72:78)
sts. Cont straight until Sleeve measures
20(24:28)cm/8 (9½:11)in from beg.
Cast off.

KEY

☐ Cream (A)
☒ Black

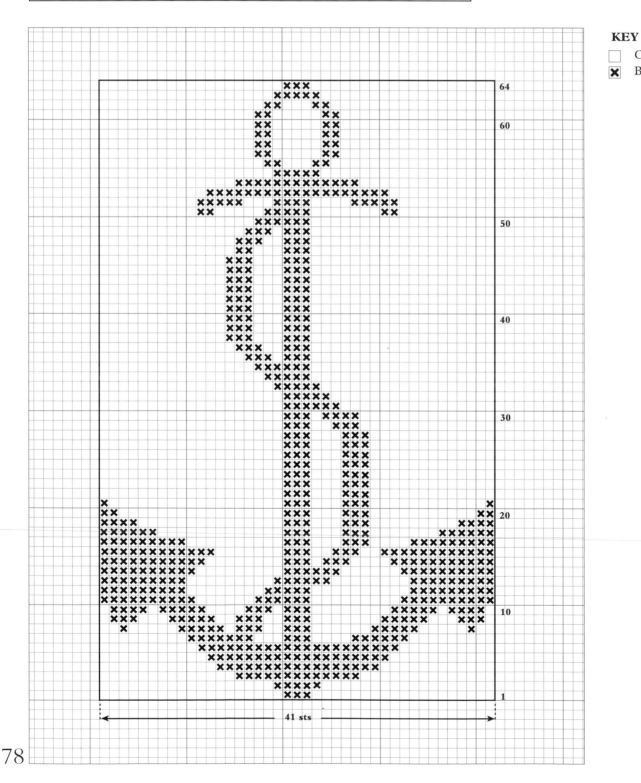

41 sts

64
60
50
40
30
20
10
1

78

NECKBAND

Join right shoulder seam.
With 3¾mm (No 9/US 4) needles, A and right side facing, k up 11(15:16) sts down left front neck, k centre front neck sts inc 3 sts, k up 11(15:16) sts up right front neck, k back neck sts inc 3(2:5) sts. 82(97:106) sts.
Next row K0(1:0), [p2, k1, p4, k1] to last 2(0:2) sts, p2(0:2).
Next row K2(0:2), [p1, C4F, p1, k2] to last 0(1:0) st, p0(1:0).
Next row K0(1:0), [p2, k1, p4, k1] to last 2(0:2) sts, p2(0:2).
Next row K2(0:2), [p1, k4, p1, k2] to last 0(1:0) st, p0(1:0).
Rep last 4 rows 1(2:2) times more, then work first 3 rows again. Cast off in patt.

TO MAKE UP

Join left shoulder and neckband seam. Sew on sleeves, placing centre of sleeves to shoulder seams. Join side and sleeve seams.

AUTHOR'S ACKNOWLEDGEMENTS

I would like to thank the following knitters for their invaluable skill: Pat Church, Connie Critchell, Tina Egleton, Jaqui Halstead, Penny Hill, Shirley Kennet, Maisie Lawrence, Frances Wallace, Betty Webb.

Thank you to Bette Anne Lampers of Snohomish, W.A. who I met at the Stitches show in San Francisco and who inspired me to attempt the Entrelac Sweater.

I am extremely grateful to Tina Egleton for her expertise and dedication in checking the patterns and to Karen McCarteney for her perfect styling and Alison Walsh for helping on the shoot.

Thanks must also go to my wonderful agent Heather Jeeves and to Cindy Richards and Kate Haxell for giving me the opportunity to work on this project.

Special thanks to the children and their families: Edie, Ella, Eleanor, Josiah, Josh and Samuel, Kitty, Max, Rene, Soloman, Selga and Quito.

Stockists/Distributors

STOCKISTS/SUPPLIERS

For overseas stockists and mail-order information please contact:

Canada
Diamond Yarn,
9697 St Laurent,
Montreal,
Quebec, H3L 2N1.
Tel: 514 388 6188
Diamond Yarn,
1450 Lodestar
Unit 4,
Toronto,
Ontario, M3J 3C1.
Tel: 416 636 1212

Demark
Ruzicka,
Hydesbyvej 27,
DK4990 Sakskoing.
Tel: 54 70 78 04

France
Elle Tricot,
52 Rue Principale,
67300 Schiltigheim.
Tel: 88 62 65 31

Germany
Wolle & Design,
Wolfshovener Strasse 76,
52428 Julich-Stetternich.
Tel: 02461/54735

Holland
Henk & Henrietta Beukers,
Dorpsstraat 9,
NL 5327 AR Hurwenen.
Tel: 0418 661764

Hong Kong
East Unity Company Ltd,
Rm 902,
Block A,
Kailey Industrial Centre,
12 Fung Yip Street,
Chair Wan.
Tel: 852 2869 7110

Iceland
Storkurinn,
Kjorgardi,
Laugavegi 59,
ICE 101.
Tel: 551 82 58

Italy
Victoriana,
Via Fratelli Pioli 14,
Rivoli,
(TO).
Tel: 011 95 32 142

Japan
Diakeito Co Ltd,
2-3-11 Senba-Higashi,
Minoh City,
Osaka 562.
Tel: 0727 27 6604

Norway
Eureka,
PO Box 357,
N 1401 Ski.
Tel: 64 86 55 40

Sweden
Wincent,
Sveavagen 94,
113 50 Stockholm.
Tel: 08673 70 60

UK
Rowan Yarns,
Green Mill Lane,
Holmfirth,
West Yorkshire HD7 1RW.
Tel: 01484 681881

USA
Westminster Fibers Inc,
5 Northern Boulevard,
Amherst,
New Hampshire 03031.
Tel: (603) 886 5041/5043.
Email: WFIBERATAOL.COM